Preface

This book is your companion on a journey through the intricate and dynamic world of Microsoft SQL Server, an open-source relational database management system that has captivated the hearts of developers, database administrators, and businesses worldwide.

In a data-driven era where information is the lifeblood of organizations, mastering a robust and versatile database system like Microsoft SQL Server is of paramount importance. This book is tailored to meet the diverse needs of readers, whether you're taking your first steps into the realm of databases or you're an experienced database professional looking to deepen your Microsoft SQL Server expertise.

This book covers a wide range of topics, starting with the foundational concepts of databases and gradually progressing to advanced techniques and emerging trends. Here's a glimpse of what you can expect:

1. Clarity and Depth: We break down complex concepts into manageable pieces, ensuring you can grasp the intricacies of Microsoft SQL Server while building a strong foundation of understanding.
2. Practical Experience: Real-world examples and hands-on exercises help you apply Microsoft SQL Server concepts in practical scenarios, from designing efficient databases to optimizing performance.
3. Comprehensive Coverage: Whether you're interested in SQL queries, database design, stored procedures, or advanced topics like replication and cloud integration, this book covers it all.
4. Best Practices: Throughout the book, we emphasize best practices for Microsoft SQL Server development, administration, and security.
5. A Learning Journey: We've structured the content to take you from Microsoft SQL Server basics to advanced techniques, allowing you to grow your skills at your own pace.

As you navigate through these pages, you'll find the collective wisdom of experienced database professionals, developers, and Microsoft SQL Server enthusiasts who have contributed to this comprehensive resource.

We'd like to express our gratitude to the Microsoft SQL Server community, whose passion and dedication have played an instrumental role in shaping this book. We'd also like to thank our families, friends, and colleagues for their unwavering support throughout this endeavour.

We believe that this book will be a valuable resource on your journey to becoming a Microsoft SQL Server master. Whether you're a student, a professional, or an enthusiast, we hope this book equips you with the knowledge and skills you need to harness the full potential of Microsoft SQL Server.

Thank you for choosing this book as your guide to the fascinating world of Microsoft SQL Server. Let's embark on this Microsoft SQL Server adventure together!

Table of Contents

Experiment 1: Creating Databases and Tables

Create the Database **CompanyDatabase** in SQL Server. In the Database **CompanyDatabase** create 2 tables **EmployeeInfo** and **EmployeePosition** with the details as below:

EmployeeInfo:
EmpID INT PRIMARY KEY,
EmpFname VARCHAR(50),
EmpLname VARCHAR(50),
Department VARCHAR(50),
Project VARCHAR(50),
Address VARCHAR(100),
DOB DATE,
Gender CHAR(1)

EmployeePosition:
EmpID INT,
EmpPosition VARCHAR(50),
DateOfJoining DATE,
Salary DECIMAL(10, 2)

With the following values:

EmployeeInfo Table:

EmpID	EmpFname	EmpLname	Department	Project	Address	DOB	Gender
1	Sanjay	Mehra	HR	P1	Hyderabad(HYD)	01/12/1976	M
2	Ananya	Mishra	Admin	P2	Delhi(DEL)	02/05/1968	F
3	Rohan	Diwan	Account	P3	Mumbai(BOM)	01/01/1980	M
4	Sonia	Kulkarni	HR	P1	Hyderabad(HYD)	02/05/1992	F
5	Ankit	Kapoor	Admin	P2	Delhi(DEL)	03/07/1994	M

EmployeePosition Table:

EmpID	EmpPosition	DateOfJoining	Salary
1	Manager	01/05/2022	500000
2	Executive	02/05/2022	75000
3	Manager	01/05/2022	90000
2	Lead	02/05/2022	85000
1	Executive	01/05/2022	300000

Solution:

Creating the database CompanyDatabase

```
-- Create the database
CREATE DATABASE CompanyDatabase;
USE CompanyDatabase;
```

Creating the EmployeeInfo Table:

```
-- Create EmployeeInfo table
CREATE TABLE EmployeeInfo (
    EmpID INT PRIMARY KEY,
    EmpFname VARCHAR(50),
    EmpLname VARCHAR(50),
    Department VARCHAR(50),
    Project VARCHAR(50),
    Address VARCHAR(100),
    DOB DATE,
    Gender CHAR(1)
);
```

Inserting data into EmployeeInfo table

```
INSERT INTO EmployeeInfo (EmpID, EmpFname, EmpLname, Department, Project, Address, DOB, Gender)
VALUES
    (1, 'Sanjay', 'Mehra', 'HR', 'P1', 'Hyderabad (HYD)', '1976-12-01', 'M'),
    (2, 'Ananya', 'Mishra', 'Admin', 'P2', 'Delhi (DEL)', '1968-05-02', 'F'),
    (3, 'Rohan', 'Diwan', 'Account', 'P3', 'Mumbai (BOM)', '1980-01-01', 'M'),
    (4, 'Sonia', 'Kulkarni', 'HR', 'P1', 'Hyderabad (HYD)', '1992-05-02', 'F'),
    (5, 'Ankit', 'Kapoor', 'Admin', 'P2', 'Delhi (DEL)', '1994-07-03', 'M');
```

Creating EmployeePosition table

```sql
-- Create EmployeePosition table
CREATE TABLE EmployeePosition (
    EmpID INT,
    EmpPosition VARCHAR(50),
    DateOfJoining DATE,
    Salary DECIMAL(10, 2)
);
```

Inserting data into EmployeePosition table

```sql
-- Insert data into EmployeePosition table
INSERT INTO EmployeePosition (EmpID, EmpPosition, DateOfJoining, Salary)
VALUES
    (1, 'Manager', '2022-05-01', 500000),
    (2, 'Executive', '2022-05-02', 75000),
    (3, 'Manager', '2022-05-01', 90000),
    (2, 'Lead', '2022-05-02', 85000),
    (1, 'Executive', '2022-05-01', 300000);
```

Practice Questions

1. Create a database named "SalesDB".

```sql
CREATE DATABASE SalesDB;
```

2. Create a table named "Customers" with primary key and basic columns.

```sql
CREATE TABLE Customers (
    CustomerID INT PRIMARY KEY,
    CustomerName VARCHAR(50),
    Email VARCHAR(100),
    Phone VARCHAR(20)
);
```

3. Create a table named "Orders" with a foreign key referencing "Customers".

```sql
CREATE TABLE Orders (
    OrderID INT PRIMARY KEY,
    OrderDate DATE,
    CustomerID INT,
    FOREIGN KEY (CustomerID) REFERENCES Customers(CustomerID)
);
```

4. Add a column "Address" to the "Customers" table.

```sql
ALTER TABLE Customers
ADD Address VARCHAR(100);
```

5. Create a table named "Products".

```sql
CREATE TABLE Products (
    ProductID INT PRIMARY KEY,
    ProductName VARCHAR(50),
    Price DECIMAL(10, 2)
);
```

6. Create a table named "OrderDetails" with foreign keys referencing "Orders" and "Products".

```sql
CREATE TABLE OrderDetails (
    OrderDetailID INT PRIMARY KEY,
    OrderID INT,
    ProductID INT,
    Quantity INT,
    FOREIGN KEY (OrderID) REFERENCES Orders(OrderID),
    FOREIGN KEY (ProductID) REFERENCES Products(ProductID)
);
```

7. Create a database named "InventoryDB".

```sql
CREATE DATABASE InventoryDB;
```

8. Create a table named "Suppliers" with basic columns and a primary key.

```sql
CREATE TABLE Suppliers (
    SupplierID INT PRIMARY KEY,
    SupplierName VARCHAR(50),
    ContactPerson VARCHAR(50),
    Email VARCHAR(100)
);
```

9. Create a table named "Products" in the "InventoryDB" database with a foreign key referencing "Suppliers".

```sql
USE InventoryDB;

CREATE TABLE Products (
    ProductID INT PRIMARY KEY,
    ProductName VARCHAR(50),
    SupplierID INT,
    FOREIGN KEY (SupplierID) REFERENCES Suppliers(SupplierID)
);
```

10. Create a table named "Inventory" in the "InventoryDB" database with foreign keys referencing "Products".

```sql
CREATE TABLE Inventory (
    InventoryID INT PRIMARY KEY,
    ProductID INT,
    Quantity INT,
    FOREIGN KEY (ProductID) REFERENCES Products(ProductID)
);
```

Experiment 2: Select, From and Where

For the Database **CompanyDatabase** having 2 tables **EmployeeInfo** and **EmployeePosition** with the details as below:

EmployeeInfo:
EmpID INT PRIMARY KEY,
EmpFname VARCHAR(50),
EmpLname VARCHAR(50),
Department VARCHAR(50),
Project VARCHAR(50),
Address VARCHAR(100),
DOB DATE,
Gender CHAR(1)

EmployeePosition:
EmpID INT,
EmpPosition VARCHAR(50),
DateOfJoining DATE,
Salary DECIMAL(10, 2)

With the following values:

EmployeeInfo Table:

EmpID	EmpFname	EmpLname	Department	Project	Address	DOB	Gender
1	Sanjay	Mehra	HR	P1	Hyderabad(HYD)	01/12/1976	M
2	Ananya	Mishra	Admin	P2	Delhi(DEL)	02/05/1968	F
3	Rohan	Diwan	Account	P3	Mumbai(BOM)	01/01/1980	M
4	Sonia	Kulkarni	HR	P1	Hyderabad(HYD)	02/05/1992	F
5	Ankit	Kapoor	Admin	P2	Delhi(DEL)	03/07/1994	M

EmployeePosition Table:

EmpID	EmpPosition	DateOfJoining	Salary
1	Manager	01/05/2022	500000
2	Executive	02/05/2022	75000
3	Manager	01/05/2022	90000
2	Lead	02/05/2022	85000
1	Executive	01/05/2022	300000

Perform the following Select, From, Where Statement:

1. Retrieve Employee Names and Departments:
2. Get Employee Names, Positions, and Salaries:
3. List Employees in HR Department
4. Find Employees in Hyderabad
5. Retrieve Employee Names, Positions, and Joining Dates

Solution:

1. Retrieve Employee Names and Departments:

```
SELECT EmpFname, EmpLname, Department
FROM EmployeeInfo;
```

100 %

Results | Messages

	EmpFname	EmpLname	Department
1	Sanjay	Mehra	HR
2	Ananya	Mishra	Admin
3	Rohan	Diwan	Account
4	Sonia	Kulkarni	HR
5	Ankit	Kapoor	Admin

2. Get Employee Names, Positions, and Salaries.

```
SELECT EI.EmpFname, EI.EmpLname, EP.EmpPosition, EP.Salary
FROM EmployeeInfo EI
JOIN EmployeePosition EP ON EI.EmpID = EP.EmpID;
```

100 %

Results | Messages

	EmpFname	EmpLname	EmpPosition	Salary
1	Sanjay	Mehra	Manager	500000.00
2	Ananya	Mishra	Executive	75000.00
3	Rohan	Diwan	Manager	90000.00
4	Ananya	Mishra	Lead	85000.00
5	Sanjay	Mehra	Executive	300000.00

3. List Employees in HR Department

```sql
SELECT *
FROM EmployeeInfo
WHERE Department = 'HR';
```

100 %

Results Messages

	EmpID	EmpFname	EmpLname	Department	Project	Address	DOB	Gender
1	1	Sanjay	Mehra	HR	P1	Hyderabad (HYD)	1976-12-01	M
2	4	Sonia	Kulkarni	HR	P1	Hyderabad (HYD)	1992-05-02	F

4. Find Employees in Hyderabad

```sql
SELECT *
FROM EmployeeInfo
WHERE Address LIKE '%Hyderabad%';
```

100 %

Results Messages

	EmpID	EmpFname	EmpLname	Department	Project	Address	DOB	Gender
1	1	Sanjay	Mehra	HR	P1	Hyderabad (HYD)	1976-12-01	M
2	4	Sonia	Kulkarni	HR	P1	Hyderabad (HYD)	1992-05-02	F

5. Retrieve Employee Names, Positions, and Joining Dates

```sql
SELECT EI.EmpFname, EI.EmpLname, EP.EmpPosition, EP.DateOfJoining
FROM EmployeeInfo EI
JOIN EmployeePosition EP ON EI.EmpID = EP.EmpID;
```

100 %

Results Messages

	EmpFname	EmpLname	EmpPosition	DateOfJoining
1	Sanjay	Mehra	Manager	2022-05-01
2	Ananya	Mishra	Executive	2022-05-02
3	Rohan	Diwan	Manager	2022-05-01
4	Ananya	Mishra	Lead	2022-05-02
5	Sanjay	Mehra	Executive	2022-05-01

Practice Questions

1. List Employee Names and Salaries:

```sql
SELECT EmpFname, EmpLname, Salary
FROM EmployeeInfo EI
JOIN EmployeePosition EP ON EI.EmpID = EP.EmpID;
```

Results | Messages

	EmpFname	EmpLname	Salary
1	Sanjay	Mehra	500000.00
2	Ananya	Mishra	75000.00
3	Rohan	Diwan	90000.00
4	Ananya	Mishra	85000.00
5	Sanjay	Mehra	300000.00

2. Count Employees in Each Department:

```sql
SELECT Department, COUNT(*) AS EmployeeCount
FROM EmployeeInfo
GROUP BY Department;
```

100 %

Results | Messages

	Department	EmployeeCount
1	Account	1
2	Admin	2
3	HR	2

3. Calculate Average Salary of Managers:

```sql
SELECT AVG(Salary) AS AvgManagerSalary
FROM EmployeePosition
WHERE EmpPosition = 'Manager';
```

100 %

Results | Messages

	AvgManagerSalary
1	295000.000000

4. Find the Highest Salary:

```sql
SELECT MAX(Salary) AS MaxSalary
FROM EmployeePosition;
```

100 %

Results | Messages

	MaxSalary
1	500000.00

5. List Employees Older Than 40:

```sql
SELECT EmpFname, EmpLname, DATEADD(year, 40, DOB) AS DateAfter40
FROM EmployeeInfo
WHERE DOB < DATEADD(year, -40, GETDATE());
```

100 %

Results | Messages

	EmpFname	EmpLname	DateAfter40
1	Sanjay	Mehra	2016-12-01
2	Ananya	Mishra	2008-05-02
3	Rohan	Diwan	2020-01-01

6. Retrieve Employee Names in HR Department:

```sql
SELECT EmpFname, EmpLname
FROM EmployeeInfo
WHERE EmpID IN (SELECT EmpID FROM EmployeePosition WHERE EmpPosition = 'HR');
```

100 %

Results | Messages

EmpFname	EmpLname

7. Find the Lowest Salary Among Executives:

```sql
SELECT MIN(Salary) AS MinSalary
FROM EmployeePosition
WHERE EmpPosition = 'Executive';
```

100 %

Results | Messages

	MinSalary
1	75000.00

8. List Employees in Hyderabad Working on Project P1:

```sql
SELECT EmpFname, EmpLname
FROM EmployeeInfo
WHERE EmpID IN (
    SELECT EP.EmpID
    FROM EmployeePosition EP
    JOIN EmployeeInfo EI ON EP.EmpID = EI.EmpID
    WHERE Address = 'Hyderabad(HYD)' AND Project = 'P1'
);
```

.00 %

Results | Messages

EmpFname	EmpLname

9. Count Employees with a Salary Greater Than Average:

```sql
SELECT COUNT(*) AS AboveAvgSalaryCount
FROM EmployeePosition
WHERE Salary > (
    SELECT AVG(Salary) AS AvgSalary
    FROM EmployeePosition
);
```

100 %

Results | Messages

	AboveAvgSalaryCount
1	2

10. Find Employees Who Joined Before Their Managers:

```
SELECT EmpFname, EmpLname
FROM EmployeeInfo
WHERE EmpID IN (
    SELECT EP.EmpID
    FROM EmployeePosition EP
    JOIN EmployeeInfo EI ON EP.EmpID = EI.EmpID
    WHERE EP.DateOfJoining < (
        SELECT EP2.DateOfJoining
        FROM EmployeePosition EP2
        WHERE EP2.EmpPosition = 'Manager' AND EP2.EmpID = EP.EmpID
    )
);
```

100 %

Results Messages

EmpFname	EmpLname

Experiment 3: Movies Database

Create Database Movies with tables and structures as given below:

actor:

act_id INTEGER PRIMARY KEY,
act_fname CHAR(20),
act_lname CHAR(20),
act_gender CHAR(1)

movie:

mov_id INTEGER PRIMARY KEY,
mov_title CHAR(50),
mov_year INTEGER,
mov_time INTEGER,
mov_lang CHAR(50),
mov_dt_rel DATE,
mov_rel_country CHAR(5)

movie_cast:

act_id INTEGER,
mov_id INTEGER,
role CHAR(30),
FOREIGN KEY (act_id) REFERENCES actor(act_id),
FOREIGN KEY (mov_id) REFERENCES movie(mov_id)

genres:

gen_id INTEGER PRIMARY KEY,
gen_title CHAR(20)

movie_genres:

mov_id INTEGER,
gen_id INTEGER,
FOREIGN KEY (mov_id) REFERENCES movie(mov_id),
FOREIGN KEY (gen_id) REFERENCES genres(gen_id)

rating:

mov_id INTEGER,
rev_id INTEGER,
rev_stars INTEGER,
num_o_ratings INTEGER,
FOREIGN KEY (mov_id) REFERENCES movie(mov_id)

reviewer:

rev_id INTEGER PRIMARY KEY,
rev_name CHAR(30)

movie_direction:

dir_id INTEGER,
mov_id INTEGER,
FOREIGN KEY (mov_id) REFERENCES movie(mov_id)

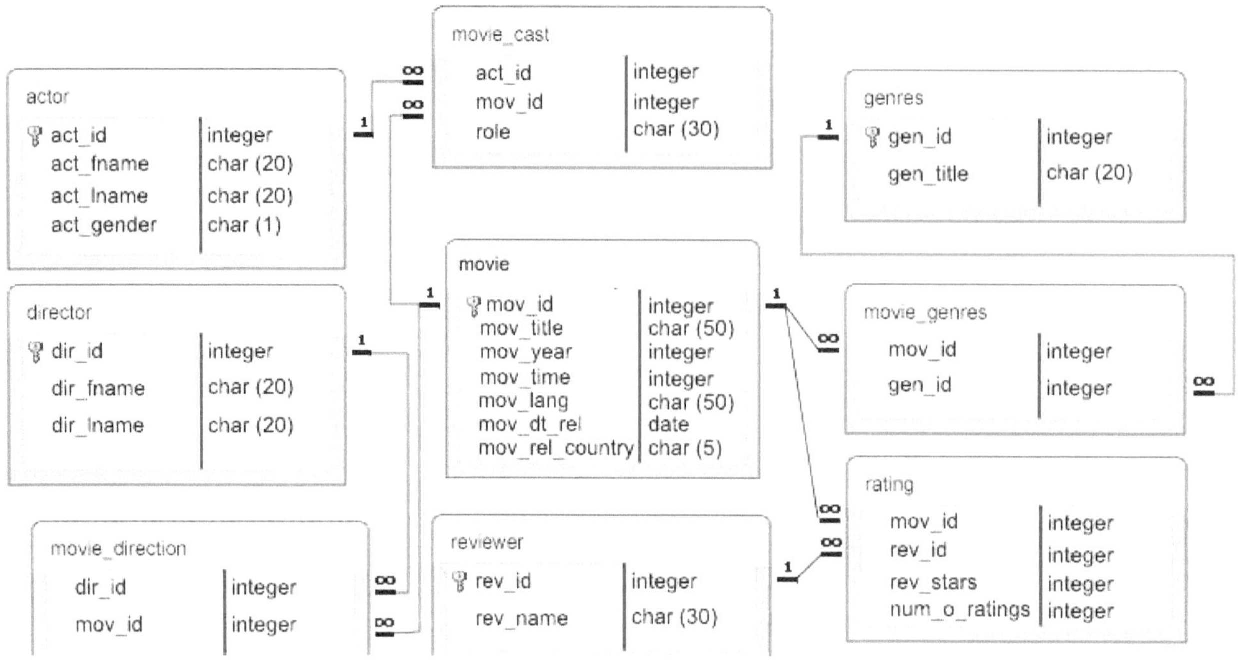

Having the values as follows:

actor:

act_id	act_fname	act_lname	act_gender
1	Shahrukh	Khan	M
2	Deepika	Padukone	F
3	Amitabh	Bachchan	M
4	Priyanka	Chopra	F
5	Salman	Khan	M
6	Kareena	Kapoor	F
7	Ranbir	Kapoor	M
8	Anushka	Sharma	F
9	Akshay	Kumar	M
10	Katrina	Kaif	F

movies:

mov_id	mov_title	mov_year	mov_time	mov_lang	mov_dt_rel	mov_rel_country
1	DDLJ	1995	189	Hindi	1995-10-20	India
2	Kabhi Khushi Kabhie Gham	2001	210	Hindi	2001-12-14	India
3	Zindagi Na Milegi Dobara	2011	152	Hindi	2011-07-15	India
4	Chak De! India	2007	153	Hindi	2007-08-10	India
5	Dil Chahta Hai	2001	185	Hindi	2001-07-24	India
6	Om Shanti Om	2007	162	Hindi	2007-11-09	India
7	3 Idiots	2009	171	Hindi	2009-12-25	India
8	Bajrangi Bhaijaan	2015	163	Hindi	2015-07-17	India
9	Kuch Kuch Hota Hai	1998	185	Hindi	1998-10-16	India
10	PK	2014	153	Hindi	2014-12-19	India

genres:

gen_id	gen_title
1	Drama
2	Romance
3	Comedy
4	Action

movie_genres:

mov_id	gen_id
1	2
2	1
3	3
4	1
5	1
6	2
7	1
8	4
9	2
10	3

rating:

mov_id	rev_id	rev_stars	num_o_ratings
1	1	5	100
2	2	4	95
3	3	4	98
4	4	4	92
5	5	4	88
6	6	5	99
7	7	4	97
8	8	4	93
9	9	5	100
19	10	4	96

reviewer:

rev_id	rev_name
1	Reviewer1
2	Reviewer2
3	Reviewer3
4	Reviewer4
5	Reviewer5
6	Reviewer6
7	Reviewer7
8	Reviewer8
9	Reviewer9
10	Reviewer10

movie_direction:

dir_id	mov_id
1	1
2	2
3	3
4	4
5	5
6	6
7	7
8	8
9	9
10	10

Solution:

Creating the database Movies:

```
CREATE DATABASE Movies
```

Creating the tables:

```sql
CREATE TABLE actor (
    act_id INTEGER PRIMARY KEY,
    act_fname CHAR(20),
    act_lname CHAR(20),
    act_gender CHAR(1)
);

CREATE TABLE movie (
    mov_id INTEGER PRIMARY KEY,
    mov_title CHAR(50),
    mov_year INTEGER,
    mov_time INTEGER,
    mov_lang CHAR(50),
    mov_dt_rel DATE,
    mov_rel_country CHAR(5)
);

CREATE TABLE movie_cast (
    act_id INTEGER,
    mov_id INTEGER,
    role CHAR(30),
    FOREIGN KEY (act_id) REFERENCES actor(act_id),
    FOREIGN KEY (mov_id) REFERENCES movie(mov_id)
);

CREATE TABLE genres (
    gen_id INTEGER PRIMARY KEY,
    gen_title CHAR(20)
);
```

```sql
CREATE TABLE movie_genres (
    mov_id INTEGER,
    gen_id INTEGER,
    FOREIGN KEY (mov_id) REFERENCES movie(mov_id),
    FOREIGN KEY (gen_id) REFERENCES genres(gen_id)
);

CREATE TABLE rating (
    mov_id INTEGER,
    rev_id INTEGER,
    rev_stars INTEGER,
    num_o_ratings INTEGER,
    FOREIGN KEY (mov_id) REFERENCES movie(mov_id)
);

CREATE TABLE reviewer (
    rev_id INTEGER PRIMARY KEY,
    rev_name CHAR(30)
);

CREATE TABLE movie_direction (
    dir_id INTEGER,
    mov_id INTEGER,
    FOREIGN KEY (mov_id) REFERENCES movie(mov_id)
);
```

Inserting values in all the tables:

```sql
-- Actors
INSERT INTO actor (act_id, act_fname, act_lname, act_gender) VALUES
(1, 'Shahrukh', 'Khan', 'M'),
(2, 'Deepika', 'Padukone', 'F'),
(3, 'Amitabh', 'Bachchan', 'M'),
(4, 'Priyanka', 'Chopra', 'F'),
(5, 'Salman', 'Khan', 'M'),
(6, 'Kareena', 'Kapoor', 'F'),
(7, 'Ranbir', 'Kapoor', 'M'),
(8, 'Anushka', 'Sharma', 'F'),
(9, 'Akshay', 'Kumar', 'M'),
(10, 'Katrina', 'Kaif', 'F');
```

```sql
-- Movies
INSERT INTO movie (mov_id, mov_title, mov_year, mov_time, mov_lang, mov_dt_rel, mov_rel_country) VALUES
(1, 'DDLJ', 1995, 189, 'Hindi', '1995-10-20', 'India'),
(2, 'Kabhi Khushi Kabhie Gham', 2001, 210, 'Hindi', '2001-12-14', 'India'),
(3, 'Zindagi Na Milegi Dobara', 2011, 153, 'Hindi', '2011-07-15', 'India'),
(4, 'Chak De! India', 2007, 153, 'Hindi', '2007-08-10', 'India'),
(5, 'Dil Chahta Hai', 2001, 185, 'Hindi', '2001-07-24', 'India'),
(6, 'Om Shanti Om', 2007, 162, 'Hindi', '2007-11-09', 'India'),
(7, '3 Idiots', 2009, 171, 'Hindi', '2009-12-25', 'India'),
(8, 'Bajrangi Bhaijaan', 2015, 163, 'Hindi', '2015-07-17', 'India'),
(9, 'Kuch Kuch Hota Hai', 1998, 185, 'Hindi', '1998-10-16', 'India'),
(10, 'PK', 2014, 153, 'Hindi', '2014-12-19', 'India');
```

```sql
-- Movie Genres
INSERT INTO genres (gen_id, gen_title) VALUES
(1, 'Drama'),
(2, 'Romance'),
(3, 'Comedy'),
(4, 'Action');
```

```sql
-- Movie Genres Mapping
INSERT INTO movie_genres (mov_id, gen_id) VALUES
(1, 2), -- DDLJ - Romance
(2, 1), -- Kabhi Khushi Kabhie Gham - Drama
(3, 3), -- Zindagi Na Milegi Dobara - Comedy
(4, 1), -- Chak De! India - Drama
(5, 1), -- Dil Chahta Hai - Drama
(6, 2), -- Om Shanti Om - Romance
(7, 1), -- 3 Idiots - Drama
(8, 4), -- Bajrangi Bhaijaan - Action
(9, 2), -- Kuch Kuch Hota Hai - Romance
(10, 3); -- PK - Comedy
```

```sql
-- Ratings
INSERT INTO rating (mov_id, rev_id, rev_stars, num_o_ratings) VALUES
(1, 1, 5, 100),
(2, 2, 4, 95),
(3, 3, 4, 98),
(4, 4, 4, 92),
(5, 5, 4, 88),
(6, 6, 5, 99),
(7, 7, 4, 97),
(8, 8, 4, 93),
(9, 9, 5, 100),
(10, 10, 4, 96);
```

```sql
-- Reviewers
INSERT INTO reviewer (rev_id, rev_name) VALUES
(1, 'Reviewer1'),
(2, 'Reviewer2'),
(3, 'Reviewer3'),
(4, 'Reviewer4'),
(5, 'Reviewer5'),
(6, 'Reviewer6'),
(7, 'Reviewer7'),
(8, 'Reviewer8'),
(9, 'Reviewer9'),
(10, 'Reviewer10');

-- Movie Direction
INSERT INTO movie_direction (dir_id, mov_id) VALUES
(1, 1), -- DDLJ
(2, 2), -- Kabhi Khushi Kabhie Gham
(3, 3), -- Zindagi Na Milegi Dobara
(4, 4), -- Chak De! India
(5, 5), -- Dil Chahta Hai
(6, 6), -- Om Shanti Om
(7, 7), -- 3 Idiots
(8, 8), -- Bajrangi Bhaijaan
(9, 9), -- Kuch Kuch Hota Hai
(10, 10); -- PK
```

Experiment 4: Perform Queries on Movies Database

Perform the following queries on the above database Movies:
1. Select all actors' first and last names:
2. Select Hindi movies released after 2010:
3. Select movie titles and their respective genres:
4. Select actors with the first name 'Shahrukh':
5. Select movies longer than 180 minutes:
6. Select movies released in 2005 and directed by the director with ID 3:
7. Count the number of movies directed by each director:
8. List directors who directed more than 2 movies:
9. List actors in ascending order of their last names:
10. List movies in descending order of their release years:
11. List actors in alphabetical order of their first names and then last names:

Solution:

Select all actors' first and last names:

```
SELECT act_fname, act_lname FROM actor;
```

100 %

Results Messages

	act_fname	act_lname
1	Shahrukh	Khan
2	Deepika	Padukone
3	Amitabh	Bachchan
4	Priyanka	Chopra
5	Salman	Khan
6	Kareena	Kapoor
7	Ranbir	Kapoor
8	Anushka	Sharma
9	Akshay	Kumar
10	Katrina	Kaif

Select Hindi movies released after 2010:

```sql
SELECT * FROM movie WHERE mov_lang = 'Hindi' AND mov_year > 2010;
```

100 %

Results Messages

	mov_id	mov_title	mov_year	mov_time	mov_lang	mov_dt_rel	mov_rel_country
1	3	Zindagi Na Milegi Dobara	2011	153	Hindi	2011-07-15	India
2	8	Bajrangi Bhaijaan	2015	163	Hindi	2015-07-17	India
3	10	PK	2014	153	Hindi	2014-12-19	India

Select movie titles and their respective genres:

```sql
SELECT m.mov_title, g.gen_title
FROM movie m JOIN movie_genres mg ON m.mov_id = mg.mov_id JOIN genres g
ON mg.gen_id = g.gen_id;
```

100 %

Results Messages

	mov_title	gen_title
1	DDLJ	Romance
2	Kabhi Khushi Kabhie Gham	Drama
3	Zindagi Na Milegi Dobara	Comedy
4	Chak De! India	Drama
5	Dil Chahta Hai	Drama
6	Om Shanti Om	Romance
7	3 Idiots	Drama
8	Bajrangi Bhaijaan	Action
9	Kuch Kuch Hota Hai	Romance
10	PK	Comedy

Select actors with the first name 'Shahrukh':

```sql
SELECT * FROM actor WHERE act_fname = 'Shahrukh';
```

100 %

Results Messages

	act_id	act_fname	act_lname	act_gender
1	1	Shahrukh	Khan	M

Select movies longer than 180 minutes:

```
SELECT * FROM movie WHERE mov_time > 180;
```

100 %

Results Messages

	mov_id	mov_title	mov_year	mov_time	mov_lang	mov_dt_rel	mov_rel_country
1	1	DDLJ	1995	189	Hindi	1995-10-20	India
2	2	Kabhi Khushi Kabhie Gham	2001	210	Hindi	2001-12-14	India
3	5	Dil Chahta Hai	2001	185	Hindi	2001-07-24	India
4	9	Kuch Kuch Hota Hai	1998	185	Hindi	1998-10-16	India

Select movies released in 2005 and directed by the director with ID 3:

```
SELECT * FROM movie_direction md JOIN movie m ON md.mov_id = m.mov_id
WHERE m.mov_year = 2005 AND md.dir_id = 3;
```

100 %

Results Messages

dir_id	mov_id	mov_id	mov_title	mov_year	mov_time	mov_lang	mov_dt_rel	mov_rel_country

Count the number of movies directed by each director:

```
SELECT md.dir_id, COUNT(m.mov_id) AS movie_count
FROM movie_direction md JOIN movie m ON md.mov_id = m.mov_id
GROUP BY md.dir_id;
```

100 %

Results Messages

	dir_id	movie_count
1	1	1
2	2	1
3	3	1
4	4	1
5	5	1
6	6	1
7	7	1
8	8	1
9	9	1
10	10	1

List directors who directed more than 2 movies:

```
SELECT md.dir_id, COUNT(m.mov_id) AS movie_count
FROM movie_direction md JOIN movie m ON md.mov_id = m.mov_id
GROUP BY md.dir_id HAVING COUNT(m.mov_id) > 2;
```

100 %

Results | Messages

dir_id	movie_count

List actors in ascending order of their last names:

```
SELECT * FROM actor ORDER BY act_lname ASC;
```

100 %

Results | Messages

	act_id	act_fname	act_lname	act_gender
1	3	Amitabh	Bachchan	M
2	4	Priyanka	Chopra	F
3	10	Katrina	Kaif	F
4	6	Kareena	Kapoor	F
5	7	Ranbir	Kapoor	M
6	5	Salman	Khan	M
7	1	Shahrukh	Khan	M
8	9	Akshay	Kumar	M
9	2	Deepika	Padukone	F
10	8	Anushka	Sharma	F

List movies in descending order of their release years:

```sql
SELECT * FROM movie ORDER BY mov_year DESC;
```

100 %

Results | Messages

	mov_id	mov_title	mov_year	mov_time	mov_lang	mov_dt_rel	mov_rel_country
1	8	Bajrangi Bhaijaan	2015	163	Hindi	2015-07-17	India
2	10	PK	2014	153	Hindi	2014-12-19	India
3	3	Zindagi Na Milegi Dobara	2011	153	Hindi	2011-07-15	India
4	7	3 Idiots	2009	171	Hindi	2009-12-25	India
5	6	Om Shanti Om	2007	162	Hindi	2007-11-09	India
6	4	Chak De! India	2007	153	Hindi	2007-08-10	India
7	5	Dil Chahta Hai	2001	185	Hindi	2001-07-24	India
8	2	Kabhi Khushi Kabhie Gham	2001	210	Hindi	2001-12-14	India
9	9	Kuch Kuch Hota Hai	1998	185	Hindi	1998-10-16	India
10	1	DDLJ	1995	189	Hindi	1995-10-20	India

List actors in alphabetical order of their first names and then last names:

```sql
SELECT * FROM actor ORDER BY act_fname, act_lname;
```

100 %

Results | Messages

	act_id	act_fname	act_lname	act_gender
1	9	Akshay	Kumar	M
2	3	Amitabh	Bachchan	M
3	8	Anushka	Sharma	F
4	2	Deepika	Padukone	F
5	6	Kareena	Kapoor	F
6	10	Katrina	Kaif	F
7	4	Priyanka	Chopra	F
8	7	Ranbir	Kapoor	M
9	5	Salman	Khan	M
10	1	Shahrukh	Khan	M

Experiment 5: Subqueries and Joins

Give solution for the following queries of **Subqueries** and **Joins:**
1. Select movies with more than the average movie duration:
2. List actors who acted in the movie 'DDLJ':
3. Inner Join: List movie titles with their respective genres:
4. Left Join: List all movies and their reviews, even if they don't have a review yet:
5. Right Join: List all reviewers and their reviewed movies, even if they haven't reviewed any movies:
6. Find movies with the same duration:
7. Select actors who acted in 'DDLJ' and 'Dangal':
8. Find movies released before the year their directors were born:

Solution:

Select movies with more than the average movie duration:

```
SELECT * FROM movie WHERE mov_time > (SELECT AVG(mov_time) FROM movie);
```

100 %

Results Messages

	mov_id	mov_title	mov_year	mov_time	mov_lang	mov_dt_rel	mov_rel_country
1	1	DDLJ	1995	189	Hindi	1995-10-20	India
2	2	Kabhi Khushi Kabhie Gham	2001	210	Hindi	2001-12-14	India
3	5	Dil Chahta Hai	2001	185	Hindi	2001-07-24	India
4	9	Kuch Kuch Hota Hai	1998	185	Hindi	1998-10-16	India

List actors who acted in the movie 'DDLJ':

```
SELECT * FROM actor WHERE act_id IN (SELECT act_id FROM movie_cast
WHERE mov_id = (SELECT mov_id FROM movie WHERE mov_title = 'DDLJ'));
```

100 %

Results Messages

act_id	act_fname	act_lname	act_gender

Inner Join: List movie titles with their respective genres:

```sql
SELECT m.mov_title, g.gen_title
FROM movie m INNER JOIN movie_genres mg ON m.mov_id = mg.mov_id
INNER JOIN genres g ON mg.gen_id = g.gen_id;
```

100 %

Results | Messages

	mov_title	gen_title
1	DDLJ	Romance
2	Kabhi Khushi Kabhie Gham	Drama
3	Zindagi Na Milegi Dobara	Comedy
4	Chak De! India	Drama
5	Dil Chahta Hai	Drama
6	Om Shanti Om	Romance
7	3 Idiots	Drama
8	Bajrangi Bhaijaan	Action
9	Kuch Kuch Hota Hai	Romance
10	PK	Comedy

Left Join: List all movies and their reviews, even if they don't have a review yet:

```sql
SELECT m.mov_title, r.rev_stars
FROM movie m LEFT JOIN rating r ON m.mov_id = r.mov_id;
```

100 %

Results | Messages

	mov_title	rev_stars
1	DDLJ	5
2	Kabhi Khushi Kabhie Gham	4
3	Zindagi Na Milegi Dobara	4
4	Chak De! India	4
5	Dil Chahta Hai	4
6	Om Shanti Om	5
7	3 Idiots	4
8	Bajrangi Bhaijaan	4
9	Kuch Kuch Hota Hai	5
10	PK	4

Right Join: List all reviewers and their reviewed movies, even if they haven't reviewed any movies:

```sql
SELECT re.rev_name, r.mov_id
FROM reviewer re RIGHT JOIN rating r ON re.rev_id = r.rev_id;
```

100 %

Results Messages

	rev_name	mov_id
1	Reviewer1	1
2	Reviewer2	2
3	Reviewer3	3
4	Reviewer4	4
5	Reviewer5	5
6	Reviewer6	6
7	Reviewer7	7
8	Reviewer8	8
9	Reviewer9	9
10	Reviewer10	10

Find movies with the same duration:

```sql
SELECT m1.mov_title, m2.mov_title
FROM movie m1 JOIN movie m2
ON m1.mov_time = m2.mov_time AND m1.mov_id != m2.mov_id;
```

100 %

Results Messages

	mov_title	mov_title
1	Zindagi Na Milegi Dobara	Chak De! India
2	Zindagi Na Milegi Dobara	PK
3	Chak De! India	Zindagi Na Milegi Dobara
4	Chak De! India	PK
5	Dil Chahta Hai	Kuch Kuch Hota Hai
6	Kuch Kuch Hota Hai	Dil Chahta Hai
7	PK	Zindagi Na Milegi Dobara
8	PK	Chak De! India

Select actors who acted in 'DDLJ' and 'Dangal':

```sql
SELECT * FROM actor WHERE act_id IN
(SELECT act_id FROM movie_cast
WHERE mov_id = (SELECT mov_id FROM movie WHERE mov_title = 'DDLJ'))
AND act_id IN (SELECT act_id FROM movie_cast
WHERE mov_id = (SELECT mov_id FROM movie WHERE mov_title = 'Dangal'));
```

100 %

Results | Messages

act_id	act_fname	act_lname	act_gender

Find movies released before the year their directors were born:

```sql
SELECT * FROM movie m WHERE m.mov_year < (
                    SELECT MIN(d.dir_id)
FROM movie_direction md JOIN director d ON md.dir_id = d.dir_id
WHERE m.mov_id = md.mov_id);
```

Practice questions:

1. List the movies directed by directors who have directed more than 2 movies.

```sql
SELECT m.mov_title, md.dir_id
FROM movie m
INNER JOIN movie_direction md ON m.mov_id = md.mov_id
INNER JOIN (
    SELECT md.dir_id
    FROM movie_direction md
    GROUP BY md.dir_id
    HAVING COUNT(md.mov_id) > 2
) AS dir_count ON md.dir_id = dir_count.dir_id;
```

2. Display the reviewers who have given the lowest rating (minimum stars) to a movie.

```sql
SELECT r.rev_name
FROM reviewer r
INNER JOIN rating rt ON r.rev_id = rt.rev_id
WHERE rt.rev_stars = (
    SELECT MIN(rt2.rev_stars)
    FROM rating rt2
);
```

100 %

Results Messages

	rev_name
1	Reviewer2
2	Reviewer3
3	Reviewer4
4	Reviewer5
5	Reviewer7
6	Reviewer8
7	Reviewer10

3. Retrieve movies and their genres where the genre is 'Action'.

```sql
SELECT m.mov_title, g.gen_title
FROM movie m
INNER JOIN movie_genres mg ON m.mov_id = mg.mov_id
INNER JOIN genres g ON mg.gen_id = g.gen_id
WHERE g.gen_title = 'Action';
```

100 %

Results Messages

	mov_title	gen_title
1	Bajrangi Bhaijaan	Action

4. List all movies that have not been rated yet.

```sql
SELECT m.mov_title
FROM movie m
LEFT JOIN rating r ON m.mov_id = r.mov_id
WHERE r.mov_id IS NULL;
```

100 %

Results Messages

mov_title

5. Display movies that have the same language and were released in the same year.

```sql
SELECT m1.mov_title, m2.mov_title
FROM movie m1
INNER JOIN movie m2 ON m1.mov_lang = m2.mov_lang
    AND m1.mov_year = m2.mov_year
    AND m1.mov_id <> m2.mov_id;
```

100 %

Results Messages

	mov_title	mov_title
1	Kabhi Khushi Kabhie Gham	Dil Chahta Hai
2	Chak De! India	Om Shanti Om
3	Dil Chahta Hai	Kabhi Khushi Kabhie Gham
4	Om Shanti Om	Chak De! India

6. Find movies with the same duration and language.

```sql
SELECT m1.mov_title, m2.mov_title
FROM movie m1
INNER JOIN movie m2 ON m1.mov_time = m2.mov_time
    AND m1.mov_lang = m2.mov_lang
    AND m1.mov_id <> m2.mov_id;
```

100 %

Results | Messages

	mov_title	mov_title
1	Zindagi Na Milegi Dobara	Chak De! India
2	Zindagi Na Milegi Dobara	PK
3	Chak De! India	Zindagi Na Milegi Dobara
4	Chak De! India	PK
5	Dil Chahta Hai	Kuch Kuch Hota Hai
6	Kuch Kuch Hota Hai	Dil Chahta Hai
7	PK	Zindagi Na Milegi Dobara
8	PK	Chak De! India

7. Select the names of reviewers who have rated a movie directed by 'Christopher Nolan'.

```sql
SELECT DISTINCT r.rev_name
FROM reviewer r
INNER JOIN rating rt ON r.rev_id = rt.rev_id
INNER JOIN movie m ON rt.mov_id = m.mov_id
INNER JOIN movie_direction md ON m.mov_id = md.mov_id
INNER JOIN movie_direction md_nolan ON md.dir_id = md_nolan.dir_id
INNER JOIN movie m_nolan ON md_nolan.mov_id = m_nolan.mov_id
WHERE m_nolan.mov_title LIKE '%Christopher Nolan%';
```

8. Retrieve movie titles along with the number of actors who acted in them.

```sql
SELECT m.mov_title, COUNT(mc.act_id) AS num_actors
FROM movie_cast mc
INNER JOIN movie m ON mc.mov_id = m.mov_id
GROUP BY m.mov_title;
```

9. Find the movies released before the first movie directed by each director.

```sql
SELECT m.mov_title
FROM movie m
INNER JOIN movie_direction md ON m.mov_id = md.mov_id
WHERE m.mov_dt_rel < (
    SELECT MIN(m_n.mov_dt_rel)
    FROM movie m_n
    INNER JOIN movie_direction md_n ON m_n.mov_id = md_n.mov_id
    WHERE md_n.dir_id = md.dir_id
);
```

10. List movies that have a greater number of reviews than the average number of reviews for all movies.

```sql
SELECT m.mov_title
FROM movie m
INNER JOIN rating rt ON m.mov_id = rt.mov_id
GROUP BY m.mov_id
HAVING COUNT(rt.rev_id) > (
    SELECT AVG(rt2.num_o_ratings)
    FROM rating rt2
);
```

Experiment 6: TOP and Like clause

Perform the following **TOP** and **LIKE** clause on the **Experiment 3** database Movies:
1. Select the first 5 movies released in Hindi:
2. List all reviewers whose names contain 'John':
3. Retrieve the top 3 longest movies:
4. Show the first 10 actors whose first names start with 'A':
5. Display movies with titles containing 'Love':
6. Get the first 5 movies released in 2000:
7. Show reviewers whose names end with 'son':
8. Retrieve the first 3 actors whose last names start with 'K':
9. Find movies with titles beginning with 'The':
10. Get the first 5 Hindi movies released after 2015:

Solution:

Select the first 5 movies released in Hindi:

```
SELECT TOP 5 mov_title
FROM movie
WHERE mov_lang = 'Hindi'
ORDER BY mov_dt_rel;
```

100 %

Results Messages

	mov_title
1	DDLJ
2	Kuch Kuch Hota Hai
3	Dil Chahta Hai
4	Kabhi Khushi Kabhie Gham
5	Chak De! India

List all reviewers whose names contain 'John':

```sql
SELECT rev_name
FROM reviewer
WHERE rev_name LIKE '%John%';
```

100 %

Results Messages

	rev_name

Retrieve the top 3 longest movies:

```sql
SELECT TOP 3 mov_title, mov_time
FROM movie
ORDER BY mov_time DESC;
```

100 %

Results Messages

	mov_title	mov_time
1	Kabhi Khushi Kabhie Gham	210
2	DDLJ	189
3	Dil Chahta Hai	185

Show the first 10 actors whose first names start with 'A':

```sql
SELECT TOP 10 act_fname, act_lname
FROM actor
WHERE act_fname LIKE 'A%'
ORDER BY act_id;
```

00 %

Results Messages

	act_fname	act_lname
1	Amitabh	Bachchan
2	Anushka	Sharma
3	Akshay	Kumar

Display movies with titles containing 'Love':

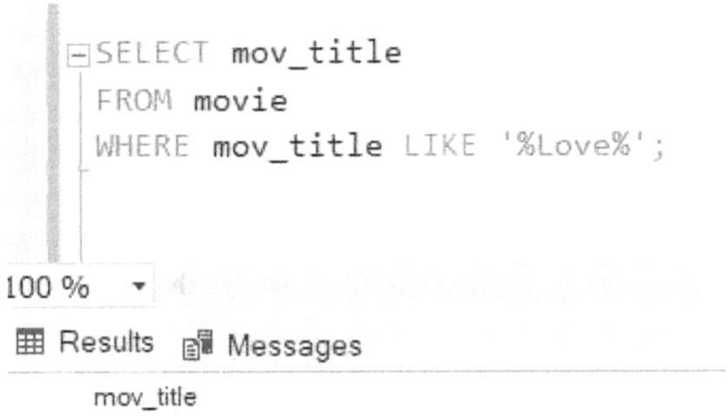

Get the first 5 movies released in 2000:

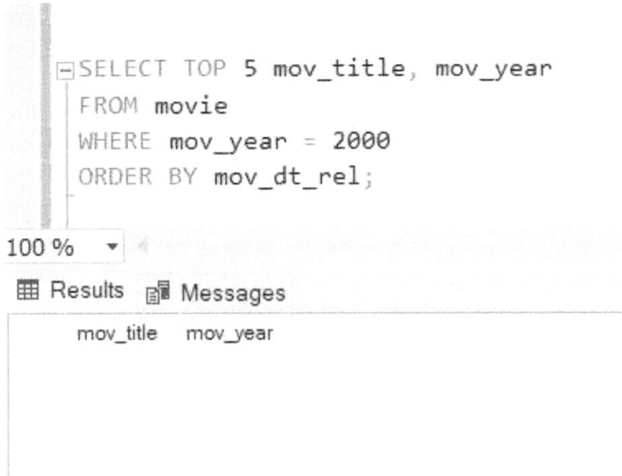

Show reviewers whose names end with 'son':

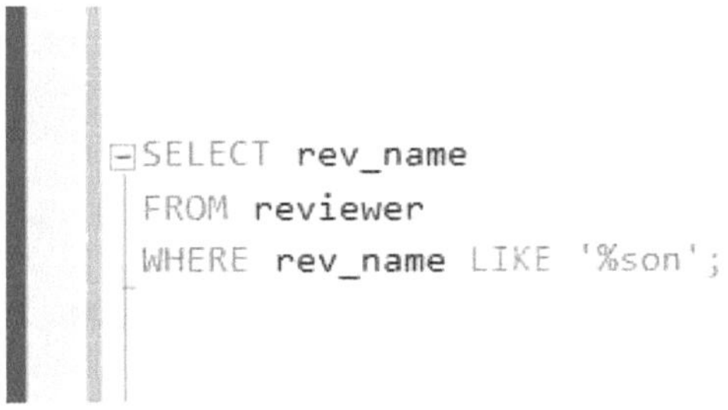

Retrieve the first 3 actors whose last names start with 'K':

```sql
SELECT TOP 3 act_fname, act_lname
FROM actor
WHERE act_lname LIKE 'K%'
ORDER BY act_id;
```

100 %

Results | Messages

	act_fname	act_lname
1	Shahrukh	Khan
2	Salman	Khan
3	Kareena	Kapoor

Find movies with titles beginning with 'The':

```sql
SELECT mov_title
FROM movie
WHERE mov_title LIKE 'The%';
```

100 %

Results | Messages

mov_title

Get the first 5 Hindi movies released after 2015:

```sql
SELECT TOP 5 mov_title, mov_year
FROM movie
WHERE mov_lang = 'Hindi' AND mov_year > 2015
ORDER BY mov_dt_rel;
```

Practice questions

1. Retrieve the movie titles and release years for all movies released in Hindi.

```sql
SELECT TOP 9 mov_title, mov_year
FROM movie
WHERE mov_lang = 'Hindi';
```

100 %

Results | Messages

	mov_title	mov_year
1	DDLJ	1995
2	Kabhi Khushi Kabhie Gham	2001
3	Zindagi Na Milegi Dobara	2011
4	Chak De! India	2007
5	Dil Chahta Hai	2001
6	Om Shanti Om	2007
7	3 Idiots	2009
8	Bajrangi Bhaijaan	2015
9	Kuch Kuch Hota Hai	1998

2. List the names of reviewers and the movies they reviewed, along with the star ratings given in their reviews.

```sql
SELECT rev_name, mov_title, rev_stars
FROM reviewer
JOIN rating ON reviewer.rev_id = rating.rev_id
JOIN movie ON rating.mov_id = movie.mov_id
ORDER BY rev_name
OFFSET 0 ROWS FETCH NEXT 10 ROWS ONLY;
```

100 %

Results | Messages

	rev_name	mov_title	rev_stars
1	Reviewer1	DDLJ	5
2	Reviewer10	PK	4
3	Reviewer2	Kabhi Khushi Kabhie Gham	4
4	Reviewer3	Zindagi Na Milegi Dobara	4
5	Reviewer4	Chak De! India	4
6	Reviewer5	Dil Chahta Hai	4
7	Reviewer6	Om Shanti Om	5
8	Reviewer7	3 Idiots	4
9	Reviewer8	Bajrangi Bhaijaan	4
10	Reviewer9	Kuch Kuch Hota Hai	5

3. Find the names of the actors who appeared in the movie with the longest duration.

```sql
WITH LongestMovie AS (
    SELECT mov_id, ROW_NUMBER() OVER (ORDER BY mov_time DESC) AS rn
    FROM movie
)
SELECT act_fname, act_lname
FROM actor
JOIN movie_cast ON actor.act_id = movie_cast.act_id
JOIN LongestMovie ON movie_cast.mov_id = LongestMovie.mov_id
WHERE rn = 1;
```

100 %

Results Messages

act_fname	act_lname

4. Display the titles of movies released after the year 2010, sorted in descending order of their release dates.

```sql
SELECT mov_title, mov_year
FROM movie
WHERE mov_year > 2010
ORDER BY mov_dt_rel DESC
OFFSET 0 ROWS FETCH NEXT 5 ROWS ONLY;
```

100 %

Results Messages

	mov_title	mov_year
1	Bajrangi Bhaijaan	2015
2	PK	2014
3	Zindagi Na Milegi Dobara	2011

5. Retrieve the names of reviewers who gave ratings of 5 stars to any movie.

```
SELECT DISTINCT rev_name
FROM reviewer
JOIN rating ON reviewer.rev_id = rating.rev_id
WHERE rev_stars = 5;
```

100 %

Results | Messages

	rev_name
1	Reviewer1
2	Reviewer6
3	Reviewer9

6. List the names of actors who appeared in a movie with the genre 'Action'.

```
SELECT DISTINCT act_fname, act_lname
FROM actor
JOIN movie_cast ON actor.act_id = movie_cast.act_id
JOIN movie_genres ON movie_cast.mov_id = movie_genres.mov_id
JOIN genres ON movie_genres.gen_id = genres.gen_id
WHERE gen_title = 'Action';
```

100 %

Results | Messages

act_fname	act_lname

7. Show the movie titles, release years, and genres for movies released before the year 2000.

```sql
SELECT mov_title, mov_year, gen_title
FROM movie
JOIN movie_genres ON movie.mov_id = movie_genres.mov_id
JOIN genres ON movie_genres.gen_id = genres.gen_id
WHERE mov_year < 2000;
```

100 %

Results | Messages

	mov_title	mov_year	gen_title
1	DDLJ	1995	Romance
2	Kuch Kuch Hota Hai	1998	Romance

8. Retrieve the names of reviewers and the number of ratings given by each reviewer.

```sql
SELECT rev_name, COUNT(*) AS num_ratings
FROM reviewer
JOIN rating ON reviewer.rev_id = rating.rev_id
GROUP BY rev_name;
```

100 %

Results | Messages

	rev_name	num_ratings
1	Reviewer1	1
2	Reviewer10	1
3	Reviewer2	1
4	Reviewer3	1
5	Reviewer4	1
6	Reviewer5	1
7	Reviewer6	1
8	Reviewer7	1
9	Reviewer8	1
10	Reviewer9	1

9. Display the movie titles and the average ratings they received.

```sql
SELECT mov_title, AVG(rev_stars) AS avg_rating
FROM movie
JOIN rating ON movie.mov_id = rating.mov_id
GROUP BY mov_title;
```

100 %

Results Messages

	mov_title	avg_rating
1	3 Idiots	4
2	Bajrangi Bhaijaan	4
3	Chak De! India	4
4	DDLJ	5
5	Dil Chahta Hai	4
6	Kabhi Khushi Kabhie Gham	4
7	Kuch Kuch Hota Hai	5
8	Om Shanti Om	5
9	PK	4
10	Zindagi Na Milegi Dobara	4

Experiment 7: Normalization and Denormalization

Present a denormalized data model and apply normalization techniques (1NF, 2NF, and 3NF) to refine it step by step.

Solution:

Let's consider a denormalized data model for a simple online bookstore where we have a single table containing multiple repeating groups. Then, we'll apply normalization techniques step by step to reach the third normal form (3NF).

Denormalized Data Model:

Consider a single table **Books** with the following attributes:

1. BookID (Primary Key)
2. Title
3. Author
4. Genre
5. Publisher
6. PublishedYear
7. Price
8. Customer1Name
9. Customer1Email
10. Customer2Name
11. Customer2Email
12. ... (Customers' details)

Steps for Normalization:

Step 1: First Normal Form (1NF)

Break down the repeating groups into separate tables.

1NF Tables:

1. Books (BookID, Title, Author, Genre, Publisher, PublishedYear, Price)
2. Customers (CustomerID, BookID, CustomerName, Email)

Step 2: Second Normal Form (2NF)

Ensure all non-key attributes are fully functionally dependent on the primary key.

2NF Tables:

1. Books (BookID, Title, Author, Genre, Publisher, PublishedYear, Price)
2. Customers (CustomerID, CustomerName, Email)
3. BookCustomers (BookID, CustomerID)

Step 3: Third Normal Form (3NF)

Eliminate transitive dependencies.

3NF Tables:

1. Books (BookID, Title, Author, Genre, Publisher, PublishedYear, Price)
2. Authors (AuthorID, AuthorName)
3. Customers (CustomerID, CustomerName, Email)
4. BookAuthors (BookID, AuthorID)
5. BookCustomers (BookID, CustomerID)

This structure ensures data integrity, minimizes redundancy, and allows for easier data management by organizing the data into related tables. Each table represents a distinct entity, and relationships are established through keys to maintain the database in the third normal form.

Explain the rationale behind each normalization form achieved.

Solution:

let's break down the rationale behind each normalization form achieved in the solution:

First Normal Form (1NF):

Rationale:

1. Elimination of Repeating Groups: In the denormalized model, customer details were stored as repeating groups (Customer1Name, Customer1Email, Customer2Name, Customer2Email, etc.) within the **Books** table.
2. Atomicity: To adhere to 1NF, these repeating groups were separated into a dedicated **Customers** table. Each customer detail is stored as a separate row, ensuring atomicity.

Second Normal Form (2NF):
Rationale:
1. Functional Dependency: 1NF was established by breaking down repeating groups, but certain attributes still depended only on a part of the primary key (**BookID** in **Books** table).
2. Further Decomposition: To achieve 2NF, the **Customers** table was separated from **Books**, ensuring all non-key attributes are dependent on the primary key (CustomerID, BookID).

Third Normal Form (3NF):
Rationale:
1. Eliminating Transitive Dependencies: In the 2NF structure, there was a transitive dependency between **Books** and **Authors**. The **Author** attribute was dependent on **BookID**.
2. Decomposition for Dependency Removal: To adhere to 3NF, the **Author** attribute was placed into a separate **Authors** table. This action eliminated the transitive dependency, ensuring that non-prime attributes are only dependent on the primary key. Now, **Books** and **Authors** are independent entities, and relationships are established through **BookAuthors**.
Overall Objective:
The primary goal of normalization is to reduce redundancy, ensure data integrity, and optimize database structure for efficient querying and maintenance. Achieving higher normal forms, like 2NF and 3NF, ensures that each table is logically organized and minimizes data duplication. This, in turn, facilitates easier updates, deletions, and insertions while preventing anomalies like insertion, update, and deletion anomalies.

Real-world Application:
1. Take a practical scenario (e.g., inventory management) and design an unnormalized data model.
2. Normalize the model to ensure it meets at least the third normal form (3NF) requirements.

Solution:

Practical Scenario: Library Management System
Unnormalized Data Model (Before Normalization):
Consider a denormalized database schema for a library management system:
Books Table:
1. BookID (Primary Key)
2. Title
3. Author
4. Genre
5. Publisher
6. YearPublished
7. ISBN
8. CopiesAvailable

Members Table:
1. MemberID (Primary Key)
2. Name
3. Email
4. Phone
5. Address
6. DateJoined
7. BooksBorrowed
Normalization Process:

First Normal Form (1NF):

1. Books Table:
2. Separate repeating groups such as multiple authors or genres into distinct rows.
3. Create a new **Authors** table with **AuthorID** (Primary Key) and **AuthorName**.
4. Similarly, create a **Genres** table with **GenreID** (Primary Key) and **GenreName**.
5. Members Table:
6. Books borrowed should be in separate rows to eliminate repeating groups.
7. Create a new table **BorrowedBooks** with columns **MemberID**, **BookID**, and **BorrowedDate**.

Second Normal Form (2NF):
1. Books Table:
2. Ensure all non-key attributes are fully functionally dependent on the entire primary key.
3. Separate publisher details into a separate **Publishers** table with **PublisherID**, **PublisherName**, **PublisherAddress**, etc.
4. Members Table:
5. The **BooksBorrowed** attribute is dependent only on **MemberID** and not on the entire primary key.
6. Move this attribute to the **BorrowedBooks** table.

Third Normal Form (3NF):
1. Books Table:
2. Analyze transitive dependencies. For instance, **Genre** might be indirectly dependent on **BookID** through **Author**.
3. Normalize the **Genre** attribute by removing it from the **Books** table and linking it to **BookID** via the **BookGenres** table.

Sample Queries:
1. Retrieve All Books by an Author:
2. Unnormalized: SELECT * FROM Books WHERE Author = 'AuthorName';
3. Normalized: SELECT * FROM Books WHERE BookID IN (SELECT BookID FROM Authors WHERE AuthorName = 'AuthorName');
4. Get Books Borrowed by a Member:
5. Unnormalized: SELECT * FROM Members WHERE MemberID = 'MemberID';
6. Normalized: SELECT * FROM BorrowedBooks WHERE MemberID = 'MemberID';
7. Find Books in a Particular Genre:
8. Unnormalized: SELECT * FROM Books WHERE Genre = 'GenreName';
9. Normalized: SELECT * FROM Books WHERE BookID IN (SELECT BookID FROM BookGenres WHERE GenreID = 'GenreID');

This normalization process ensures each table represents a distinct entity and establishes relationships between them, leading to better data consistency and reduced redundancy in a library management system.

Practice Questions:

1. Given an unnormalized table, normalize it to 3NF, showing each step.

normalizing a table to the third normal form (3NF) typically involves these steps:

Unnormalized Table:

Consider a table **EmployeeInfo** with the following attributes:

EmployeeID	EmployeeName	Department	DepartmentHead	Location	Salary
101	John Doe	HR	Sarah Johnson	New York	60000
102	Jane Smith	Marketing	Michael Brown	Los Angeles	55000
103	Alex Johnson	HR	Sarah Johnson	New York	62000
104	Alice Lee	Development	Chris Thompson	San Francisco	65000

Steps for Normalization:

Identify Functional Dependencies:

1. EmployeeID → EmployeeName, Department, DepartmentHead, Location, Salary
2. Department → DepartmentHead

3. Location → City

Remove Repeating Groups:

Create separate tables for unique entities.

Employee Table (1NF):

EmployeeID	EmployeeName	Department	Location	Salary
101	John Doe	HR	New York	60000
102	Jane Smith	Marketing	Los Angeles	55000
103	Alex Johnson	HR	New York	62000
104	Alice Lee	Development	San Francisco	65000

Department Table (2NF):

Department	DepartmentHead
HR	Sarah Johnson
Marketing	Michael Brown
Development	Chris Thompson

Location Table (3NF):

Location	City
New York	New York
Los Angeles	Los Angeles
San Francisco	San Francisco

Remove Transitive Dependencies:

No transitive dependencies exist in this case.

Now, the **EmployeeInfo** table has been normalized into 3NF with separate tables for employees, departments, and locations, eliminating redundant data and ensuring data integrity.

2. Identify and explain the potential functional dependencies in a given table.

Functional dependencies in a table represent relationships between attributes, where the value of one attribute determines the value of another within the same table. They help define how data is organized and can be crucial for normalization.

For instance, consider a table **StudentCourses** with attributes **StudentID**, **CourseID**, **StudentName**, **CourseName**, **EnrollmentYear**, and **Instructor**.

1. Identifying Potential Functional Dependencies:
2. StudentID → StudentName, EnrollmentYear
3. CourseID → CourseName, Instructor
4. (StudentID, CourseID) → EnrollmentYear, CourseName, Instructor
5. Explanation:
6. **StudentID** uniquely determines the **StudentName** and **EnrollmentYear**. A student's ID correlates with their name and the year of enrollment.
7. Similarly, **CourseID** uniquely determines the **CourseName** and **Instructor**. Each course ID is associated with a specific course name and instructor.
8. The combination of **StudentID** and **CourseID** together determines the **EnrollmentYear**, **CourseName**, and **Instructor**. It represents the enrollment details of a student in a specific course.

Functional dependencies guide the process of normalization by identifying the relationships among attributes. These dependencies help in eliminating redundancy and anomalies while organizing data into normalized forms, ensuring better data integrity and management.

3. Demonstrate the process of decomposing a table that violates 3NF into multiple tables that conform to 3NF.

Let's consider a table that violates the third normal form (3NF) and decompose it into multiple tables that adhere to 3NF.

Example Table (Violation of 3NF):

Consider a table **EmployeeDetails**:

EmployeeID	EmployeeName	Department	Manager	ManagerDepartment
1	John	HR	Alice	HR
2	Alice	HR	NULL	NULL
3	Bob	Sales	John	HR

This table violates 3NF due to transitive dependencies. **Manager** and **ManagerDepartment** depend on **EmployeeName**, which itself depends on **EmployeeID** and **Department**.

Decomposing into 3NF:

We'll decompose the table into multiple tables to eliminate transitive dependencies.

EmployeeInformation Table:

EmployeeID	EmployeeName	DepartmentID
1	John	1
2	Alice	1
3	Bob	2

DepartmentDetails Table:

DepartmentID	Department
1	HR
2	Sales

EmployeeManagement Table:

EmployeeID	ManagerID
1	2
2	NUL
3	1

Explanation:

1. **EmployeeInformation:** Contains basic employee information and the associated department ID.
2. **DepartmentDetails:** Stores department names along with their unique IDs.
3. **EmployeeManagement:** Establishes a relationship between employees and their managers using their respective IDs.

By decomposing the original table into these tables, we've eliminated the transitive dependency issues present in the initial table. Now, each table represents a distinct entity and adheres to the third normal form (3NF).

4. Describe de-normalization and when it's applicable in database design.

De-normalization is the process of intentionally introducing redundancy into a database by combining tables to optimize query performance or simplify complex data models. It involves relaxing normalization principles to increase data retrieval speed, reduce the number of joins, or improve overall system performance.

When is De-normalization Applicable?

1. **Performance Optimization:** In scenarios where a highly normalized database structure leads to slow query performance due to frequent joins across multiple tables, de-normalization can be employed. It reduces the need for complex joins and can enhance query execution speed.
2. **Read-Heavy Applications:** For systems where there's a high volume of read operations compared to write operations, de-normalization can be beneficial. It precalculates results and reduces the computational load during queries.
3. **Reporting and Analytics:** De-normalization is often used in data warehousing or reporting systems. It simplifies complex queries by aggregating data into fewer tables, making reporting operations more efficient.
4. **Caching or Materialized Views:** Storing precomputed or aggregated data in a de-normalized structure can serve as a form of caching, allowing quicker access to frequently accessed information.

Applicability Considerations:

1. Trade-Offs: De-normalization introduces redundancy, which can lead to increased storage requirements and data inconsistency issues during updates or inserts.
2. Use Case Specific: It's crucial to assess the specific use case and performance requirements before opting for de-normalization. Not all databases benefit from this technique.
3. Maintenance Complexity: De-normalized structures might be harder to maintain, especially when ensuring data consistency and integrity across redundant data.
4. Backup and Recovery: Since de-normalization involves redundant data, backup and recovery processes might become more complex and time-consuming.
Conclusion:
De-normalization is a technique used strategically in database design to enhance performance in specific scenarios. However, it comes with trade-offs regarding data integrity, storage, and maintenance complexities. It's essential to weigh these considerations against the performance gains before implementing de-normalization in a database design.

5. Explain scenarios where de-normalization can improve performance but might introduce redundancy.

De-normalization is a technique used to optimize database performance at the cost of introducing redundancy. Here are scenarios where de-normalization can enhance performance but may lead to redundancy:
1. Frequent Joins Impacting Performance:
2. Scenario: In highly normalized databases, frequent joins across multiple tables can significantly impact query performance.
3. De-normalization Impact: Combining related tables or introducing redundant data can reduce the need for these complex joins, improving query speed.
4. Redundancy Concern: Duplicate data might exist across tables, leading to potential inconsistencies during updates or inserts.
5. Read-Heavy Workloads:
6. Scenario: Systems with a high volume of read operations compared to writes often face performance challenges due to the overhead of multiple joins.
7. De-normalization Impact: Creating consolidated tables or materialized views can speed up query execution by precalculating results.
8. Redundancy Concern: Aggregated or derived data stored in de-normalized structures may lead to redundancy if not properly maintained.
9. Reporting and Analytics:
10. Scenario: Reporting systems often require complex queries involving aggregations or extensive joins.
11. De-normalization Impact: Creating denormalized reporting tables or using materialized views simplifies queries, improving reporting performance.
12. Redundancy Concern: Storing aggregated data might introduce redundancy compared to the normalized source data.
13. Caching and Performance Improvement:
14. Scenario: Systems serving frequently accessed data may benefit from caching to speed up data retrieval.
15. De-normalization Impact: Pre-calculating and storing frequently accessed data in a de-normalized cache or summary tables enhances performance.
16. Redundancy Concern: Cached or summarized data might exist redundantly compared to the original source data.
17. Historical Data and Snapshots:
18. Scenario: Storing historical snapshots or versioned data for analytical purposes or auditing.
19. De-normalization Impact: Maintaining separate historical tables or snapshots for specific periods can streamline historical queries.
20. Redundancy Concern: Duplicate or redundant data across versions or snapshots might be stored for historical purposes.
While de-normalization can significantly improve performance in these scenarios, it's essential to carefully manage and reconcile the redundancy introduced to avoid data inconsistencies and maintain data integrity. Regular maintenance and update strategies are crucial to mitigate potential issues arising from redundant data.

6. Compare and contrast normalization and de-normalization in terms of data integrity, storage space, and query performance.

Normalization and de-normalization are opposite strategies in database design, each with its own impact on data integrity, storage space, and query performance:

Normalization:
1. Data Integrity: Emphasizes data integrity by minimizing redundancy and dependency issues.
2. Storage Space: Typically results in efficient storage by reducing redundant data, which may lead to less storage space.
3. Query Performance: Might lead to more complex queries due to distributed data across normalized tables. Joins and queries could become slower, especially when dealing with large datasets, as they require multiple table joins.

De-normalization:
1. Data Integrity: Might introduce redundancy, raising the risk of data inconsistencies if not carefully managed.
2. Storage Space: Can potentially increase storage requirements due to redundant data storage.
3. Query Performance: Generally improves query performance by reducing the need for complex joins and enabling faster data retrieval, especially for read-heavy operations. Aggregated or pre-joined data simplifies queries, leading to faster execution.

Comparison:
1. Data Integrity: Normalization prioritizes data integrity by minimizing redundancy and dependency issues. De-normalization, while optimizing performance, might compromise data integrity due to redundant data storage.
2. Storage Space: Normalization often optimizes storage by eliminating redundant data. De-normalization can increase storage requirements due to redundant data storage.
3. Query Performance: Normalization can lead to slower queries due to multiple table joins, especially with large datasets. De-normalization generally enhances query performance by simplifying queries, reducing joins, and enabling faster data retrieval.

In summary, while normalization aims to maintain data integrity and optimize storage, it can lead to more complex queries. De-normalization sacrifices some data integrity to improve query performance, particularly in read-heavy environments, by reducing joins and enabling faster data retrieval. The choice between the two strategies often depends on the specific requirements of the application and the trade-offs between data integrity and performance.

7. Provide examples where de-normalization could lead to faster query execution and analyze potential downsides in terms of data consistency.

De-normalization can enhance query performance in various scenarios:
1. Aggregate Data for Reporting:
2. Example: Creating a summary table that aggregates data (like total sales per month) from multiple normalized tables.
3. Query Optimization: Simplifies and speeds up queries for reporting purposes by eliminating the need for complex joins and computations.
4. Reducing Joins for Read-Heavy Operations:
5. Example: Adding redundant data in a single table that was previously spread across multiple normalized tables.
6. Query Optimization: Reduces join operations, making read-heavy queries faster and more straightforward.
7. Caching Frequently Accessed Data:
8. Example: Creating a denormalized cache table with frequently accessed data.
9. Query Optimization: Avoids complex joins and computations for data that's frequently accessed, improving overall query performance.

Potential downsides of de-normalization in terms of data consistency:
1. Data Redundancy and Update Anomalies:
2. Issue: Introducing redundant data might lead to inconsistencies when updating or modifying data.
3. Example: Updating a value in one place and forgetting to update it in all redundant copies.
4. Increased Complexity in Maintenance:
5. Issue: De-normalized structures might become harder to maintain and update.

6. Example: Inconsistent updates across redundant copies of data could lead to data integrity issues.
7. Storage Overhead:
8. Issue: De-normalized data can consume more storage due to redundant copies.
9. Example: Storing the same information in multiple locations to speed up queries might increase storage requirements.
Balancing the benefits of improved query performance against the risks of potential data inconsistencies is critical when considering de-normalization. Careful planning, maintenance, and implementation are necessary to mitigate the downsides and ensure data integrity.

8. Discuss real-world applications where de-normalization was employed to improve database performance, highlighting the trade-offs involved.

De-normalization is often employed in various real-world scenarios to optimize database performance, although it introduces certain trade-offs. Here are a few examples:
1. Data Warehousing and Reporting:
2. Application: In data warehousing environments, de-normalization is common to accelerate complex analytical queries. Summary tables or aggregated data are created from normalized transactional data.
3. Trade-offs: Increases storage requirements due to redundant data. Maintenance complexity arises when ensuring consistency between original and de-normalized data.
4. Content Management Systems (CMS):
5. Application: CMS platforms may de-normalize data for faster content retrieval. Storing additional metadata or redundant data for frequently accessed content can speed up searches.
6. Trade-offs: The need for synchronization between original and de-normalized data sources to maintain consistency and integrity.
7. E-commerce Platforms:
8. Application: Product catalog management systems may de-normalize product information (like prices or attributes) for faster search and display.
9. Trade-offs: Possibility of inconsistent data if updates are not applied uniformly across all copies of the de-normalized data. Increased storage requirements due to redundant information.
10. Online Analytical Processing (OLAP) Systems:
11. Application: OLAP databases often de-normalize data to support complex analytical queries. Aggregated tables or materialized views are created to speed up multidimensional analysis.
12. Trade-offs: Introducing redundancy might lead to inconsistencies if updates aren't handled carefully. Maintenance challenges due to data synchronization.
13. Caching Mechanisms:
14. Application: Caching frequently accessed data in a denormalized format (like in-memory or NoSQL databases) can significantly improve response times for applications.
15. Trade-offs: Potential inconsistency between cached and source data. Increased memory requirements for caching purposes.

In these scenarios, de-normalization is employed to optimize read-heavy operations, enhance query performance, and reduce response times. However, it necessitates careful consideration of trade-offs, such as increased storage requirements, complexity in maintaining consistency, and potential data integrity issues. Successful implementations require balancing performance gains against the risks associated with redundant data.

Experiment 8: Constraints and Indexes

Constraints and Indexes:
1. Create a table 'Employees' with fields like EmployeeID, EmployeeName, and Email. Apply constraints such as NOT NULL, UNIQUE, PRIMARY KEY, FOREIGN KEY to these fields appropriately.
2. Design a scenario where you have a large 'Orders' table. Create an index on the 'OrderDate' field. Explain the process and the impact of indexing on query performance.
3. Develop a view named 'MonthlySales' that displays the total sales for each month from a 'Sales' table. Show how this view can be used to retrieve monthly sales easily.

Solution:
1)

```
-- Creating Employees table
CREATE TABLE Employees (
    EmployeeID INT PRIMARY KEY, -- Primary Key constraint
    EmployeeName VARCHAR(50) NOT NULL, -- NOT NULL constraint
    Email VARCHAR(100) UNIQUE -- UNIQUE constraint
);

-- Creating a new table 'Departments' with DepartmentID and DepartmentName
CREATE TABLE Departments (
    DepartmentID INT PRIMARY KEY,
    DepartmentName VARCHAR(50)
);

-- Adding FOREIGN KEY constraint to 'Employees' table
ALTER TABLE Employees
ADD DepartmentID INT, -- Foreign Key column
CONSTRAINT FK_Employee_Department FOREIGN KEY (DepartmentID)
    REFERENCES Departments(DepartmentID);
```

Explanation:
1. EmployeeID INT PRIMARY KEY: Defines the EmployeeID field as the primary key.
2. EmployeeName VARCHAR(50) NOT NULL: Specifies the EmployeeName field as NOT NULL, ensuring it cannot have null values.
3. Email VARCHAR(100) UNIQUE: Sets the Email field as UNIQUE, preventing duplicate email entries.
4. ALTER TABLE Employees ADD DepartmentID INT: Adds a new column 'DepartmentID' to the 'Employees' table to create a link to the 'Departments' table.
5. CONSTRAINT FK_Employee_Department FOREIGN KEY (DepartmentID) REFERENCES Departments(DepartmentID): Creates a FOREIGN KEY constraint that references the 'DepartmentID' field in the 'Departments' table. This constraint ensures referential integrity between the 'Employees' and 'Departments' tables.

This SQL script sets up the 'Employees' table with appropriate constraints, including NOT NULL, UNIQUE, PRIMARY KEY, and FOREIGN KEY as specified.

2) Let's consider a scenario where there's a large 'Orders' table in a retail database that contains various fields like OrderID, CustomerID, OrderDate, TotalAmount, and so on.

Index Creation Process:

To create an index on the 'OrderDate' field in the 'Orders' table:

```
-- Creating an index on OrderDate field
CREATE INDEX IX_OrderDate ON Orders(OrderDate);
```

Impact on Query Performance:

1. Improvement in Query Speed:
2. Queries involving the 'OrderDate' field will likely experience improved performance, especially those that use 'OrderDate' as a filter or in the 'WHERE', 'JOIN', 'GROUP BY', or 'ORDER BY' clauses.
3. For instance, queries like finding orders on specific dates, sorting orders by date, or aggregating orders by date will benefit from this index.
4. Reduced Scan Time:
5. With an index on 'OrderDate', the query optimizer can use it to quickly locate rows that match the specified 'OrderDate' criteria without scanning the entire table.
6. This reduces the disk I/O and processing time required to retrieve the relevant rows, leading to faster query execution.
7. Cost of Index Maintenance:
8. However, it's essential to consider that maintaining indexes incurs additional overhead during data modifications (inserts, updates, deletes).
9. Each time the 'OrderDate' field is modified, the index needs to be updated, potentially impacting the performance of write operations.
10. Applicability of Index Usage:
11. The effectiveness of an index depends on various factors like the cardinality of the indexed field, the selectivity of queries, database size, hardware, etc.
12. If queries rarely filter or sort by 'OrderDate', the overhead of maintaining the index might not justify the performance gains.
13. Monitor and Evaluate Performance:
14. Regularly monitor query performance before and after index creation to ensure the expected performance gains.
15. Consider the overall database workload and assess whether the benefits of the index outweigh the overhead.

In summary, while indexing 'OrderDate' can significantly enhance query performance for certain types of queries, it's crucial to weigh the trade-offs between improved query speed and the overhead of index maintenance, especially in scenarios with large tables and diverse query patterns.

3) To start, let's create a 'Sales' table, insert some sample data, and then create a view named 'MonthlySales' that displays the total sales for each month. Assuming the 'Sales' table has fields like 'SaleID', 'SaleDate', and 'Amount':

Creating the Sales Table and Inserting Sample Data:

```sql
-- Create Sales table
CREATE TABLE Sales (
    SaleID INT PRIMARY KEY,
    SaleDate DATE,
    Amount DECIMAL(10, 2)
);

-- Insert sample data into Sales table
INSERT INTO Sales (SaleID, SaleDate, Amount)
VALUES
    (1, '2023-01-15', 1500.00),
    (2, '2023-01-20', 2200.00),
    (3, '2023-02-05', 1800.00),
    (4, '2023-02-10', 3000.00),
    (5, '2023-03-08', 2500.00),
    (6, '2023-03-20', 3200.00);
```

```
100 %
Messages

(6 rows affected)

Completion time: 2023-12-14T09:57:57.8684889+05:30
```

Creating the 'MonthlySales' View:
Now, let's create a view named 'MonthlySales' that aggregates total sales for each month:

```sql
-- Create the MonthlySales view in SSMS
GO

CREATE VIEW MonthlySales AS
SELECT
    YEAR(SaleDate) AS [Year],
    MONTH(SaleDate) AS [Month],
    SUM(Amount) AS TotalSales
FROM
    Sales
GROUP BY
    YEAR(SaleDate), MONTH(SaleDate)
ORDER BY
    YEAR(SaleDate), MONTH(SaleDate);
```

Using the 'MonthlySales' View:
With the 'MonthlySales' view created, you can easily retrieve monthly sales by querying the view:

```
-- Query the MonthlySales view to retrieve monthly sales
SELECT * FROM MonthlySales;
```

This query will display the total sales for each month based on the data present in the 'Sales' table. The 'MonthlySales' view abstracts the aggregation logic, allowing users to easily access monthly sales information without the need to write complex aggregation queries repeatedly.

Practice Questions:
1. Create a view 'TopCustomers' that displays the top 10 customers based on their total purchase amounts. Can you perform updates or insertions through this view? Explain.

Creating a view that displays the top 10 customers based on their total purchase amounts can be done with a query like this:

```
CREATE VIEW TopCustomers AS
SELECT TOP 10
    CustomerID,
    SUM(PurchaseAmount) AS TotalPurchaseAmount
FROM
    Orders
GROUP BY
    CustomerID
ORDER BY
    SUM(PurchaseAmount) DESC;
```

Regarding updates or insertions through this view, it depends on various factors:
1. Updatable Views: Views can be updatable in SQL Server if certain conditions are met:
- The view is based on a single table.
- The view selects all columns of the base table.
- The view doesn't contain any aggregate functions (like **SUM**, **COUNT**, etc.) or **DISTINCT**.

However, in this scenario, the view **TopCustomers** contains aggregate functions (**SUM**) and does not cover all columns of any base table directly. So, it's not inherently updatable.
2. Trigger Updates: Even if a view is not directly updatable, you can use triggers on the base tables to update them indirectly when changes are made through the view.
3. Insertions: Generally, if a view is not updatable, insertions cannot be performed directly through the view.
In this specific case, since the **TopCustomers** view contains aggregated data (**SUM**) and does not directly map to a single base table or cover all columns of any base table, it likely won't be updatable or allow insertions directly. If modifications are necessary, it's advisable to perform them on the underlying base tables (**Orders**, **Customers**, etc.) rather than through this view.

2. Create a temporary table 'TempSales' to store sales data for a short duration. Illustrate how temporary tables are different from permanent tables in terms of scope and usage.

In SQL Server, temporary tables are created with the # symbol for local temporary tables and ## for global temporary tables. Here's an example of creating a local temporary table:

```
CREATE TABLE #TempSales (
    SaleID INT,
    SaleDate DATE,
    Amount DECIMAL(10, 2)
);
```

Temporary tables differ from permanent tables in terms of scope and usage:
1. Scope:
2. Temporary Tables: These exist only for the duration of a user session or the query execution. Local temporary tables (**#TempSales**) are only visible within the session they were created in and are automatically dropped when the session ends.
3. Permanent Tables: They persist in the database until explicitly dropped. They have broader visibility and can be accessed by multiple users and sessions.
4. Usage:
5. Temporary Tables: Typically used for storing intermediate results, temporary data, or complex calculations during a session or specific operation. They help in breaking down complex tasks into smaller steps.
6. Permanent Tables: Used for persistent storage of data that needs to be accessed across different sessions or by multiple users. They are the primary storage for application data.
7. Differences:
8. Temporary tables are often used in scenarios like data staging, complex query intermediates, or temporary data storage within a specific session or task.
9. Permanent tables are designed for long-term storage of essential data for applications or systems.

Remember, when using temporary tables:
1. They're automatically dropped when the session ends.
2. Local temporary tables are only visible within the session where they are created.
3. Global temporary tables (**##TempSales**) have a broader scope and persist until all sessions referencing them end or until explicitly dropped.

3. Compare and contrast table variables and temporary tables in SQL Server. Explain when to use each and their differences in terms of performance and scope.

Table Variables and Temporary Tables in SQL Server are both used to store and manipulate data, but they have several differences in terms of scope, usage, and performance:
1. Scope:
2. Table Variables: Limited to the batch, procedure, or function where they are defined. Their scope is narrower compared to temporary tables.
3. Temporary Tables: Have a broader scope. Local temporary tables (**#TempTables**) are visible within the session they were created in. Global temporary tables (**##TempTables**) are visible across different sessions.
4. Usage:
5. Table Variables: Useful for storing a small amount of data. They're typically used within stored procedures or functions for small-scale data manipulations or intermediate results.
6. Temporary Tables: Designed for more extensive data storage and manipulation. They're commonly used for storing larger datasets, complex intermediate results, or when extensive operations are needed.
7. Performance:
8. Table Variables: Generally have better performance for smaller datasets due to their optimized memory use. However, for larger datasets, they might not perform as well as temporary tables.
9. Temporary Tables: Offer better performance for larger datasets due to optimized statistics and execution plans. They tend to handle more data efficiently.
10. Transaction Log Usage:

11. Table Variables: Minimal logging, which can be beneficial for reducing transaction log overhead.
12. Temporary Tables: More logging compared to table variables, especially for large datasets, which might affect performance in terms of transaction log usage.
When to Use Each:
1. Table Variables: Ideal for small datasets, simple operations, or when you need to pass data between stored procedures or functions within the same scope.
2. Temporary Tables: Suitable for larger datasets, complex operations, or when you need to persist data across multiple sessions or have broader visibility within a session.
Choosing between them involves considering the size of the data, the complexity of operations, transaction log considerations, and the scope of data required. For smaller datasets or limited scope, table variables might offer better performance. For larger datasets and broader scope, temporary tables might be more appropriate.

4. Write SQL statements to add constraints to an existing table 'Products'. Apply a UNIQUE constraint on the 'ProductCode' field and a FOREIGN KEY constraint on the 'CategoryID' field.

Here are the SQL statements to add constraints to the existing 'Products' table:

```
-- Adding UNIQUE constraint on ProductCode field
ALTER TABLE Products
ADD CONSTRAINT UC_ProductCode UNIQUE (ProductCode);

-- Adding FOREIGN KEY constraint on CategoryID field
ALTER TABLE Products
ADD CONSTRAINT FK_CategoryID
FOREIGN KEY (CategoryID)
REFERENCES Categories(CategoryID);
```

These statements assume that the 'Products' table already exists, and 'ProductCode' is the column that requires a UNIQUE constraint while 'CategoryID' needs a FOREIGN KEY constraint referencing the 'CategoryID' column in the 'Categories' table. Adjust the table and column names as needed.

5. Create a scenario with a large dataset and execute queries before and after adding indexes on critical columns. Measure and compare the query execution time to demonstrate indexing benefits.

Let's consider a 'Sales' table with a substantial dataset:

```
CREATE TABLE Sales (
    SaleID INT PRIMARY KEY,
    ProductID INT,
    SaleDate DATE,
    Amount DECIMAL(10, 2),
    -- Other relevant columns
);
```

Now, let's populate the 'Sales' table with a large dataset:

```sql
-- Inserting sample data into the Sales table
INSERT INTO Sales (SaleID, ProductID, SaleDate, Amount)
SELECT
    ROW_NUMBER() OVER (ORDER BY (SELECT NULL)),
    ABS(CHECKSUM(NEWID())) % 1000 + 1, -- Random ProductID within a range
    DATEADD(DAY, -(ABS(CHECKSUM(NEWID())) % 365), GETDATE()), -- Random SaleDate within a year
    ROUND(RAND() * 1000, 2) -- Random Amount
FROM
    sys.all_objects a
CROSS JOIN
    sys.all_objects b;
```

Now, let's execute a sample query before indexing:

```sql
SET STATISTICS TIME ON;

SELECT *
FROM Sales
WHERE SaleDate BETWEEN '2022-01-01' AND '2022-12-31';

SET STATISTICS TIME OFF;
```

To measure the query execution time, use **SET STATISTICS TIME ON/OFF**.

After observing the execution time, create an index on the 'SaleDate' column:

```sql
CREATE INDEX IX_SaleDate ON Sales (SaleDate);
```

Execute the same query again after adding the index and compare the execution times. You should notice a reduction in query execution time after indexing the 'SaleDate' column due to improved data retrieval efficiency.
Remember to consider the impact of adding indexes, as they can also affect data modification operations and disk space. It's essential to evaluate trade-offs between improved query performance and potential downsides in specific scenarios.

6. Develop a complex query involving multiple joins and filters on a 'Sales' table. Rewrite the query using an existing view 'MonthlySales' and analyze the execution time difference.

Let's create a complex query involving multiple joins and filters on a 'Sales' table:

```sql
SELECT
    s.SaleID,
    p.ProductName,
    c.CategoryName,
    s.Amount,
    s.SaleDate
FROM
    Sales s
INNER JOIN
    Products p ON s.ProductID = p.ProductID
INNER JOIN
    Categories c ON p.CategoryID = c.CategoryID
WHERE
    s.SaleDate BETWEEN '2022-01-01' AND '2022-12-31'
    AND c.CategoryName = 'Electronics'
ORDER BY
    s.SaleDate DESC;
```

Now, let's rewrite this query using the existing 'MonthlySales' view:

```sql
SELECT
    s.SaleID,
    p.ProductName,
    c.CategoryName,
    s.Amount,
    s.SaleDate
FROM
    MonthlySales ms
JOIN
    Sales s ON YEAR(ms.SaleDate) = YEAR(s.SaleDate)
           AND MONTH(ms.SaleDate) = MONTH(s.SaleDate)
JOIN
    Products p ON s.ProductID = p.ProductID
JOIN
    Categories c ON p.CategoryID = c.CategoryID
WHERE
    ms.Year = 2022 -- Change the year accordingly
    AND c.CategoryName = 'Electronics'
ORDER BY
    s.SaleDate DESC;
```

To analyze the execution time difference, execute both queries and use **SET STATISTICS TIME ON/OFF**:

```
-- Query using direct joins
SET STATISTICS TIME ON;

-- Execute the query here

SET STATISTICS TIME OFF;

-- Query using the MonthlySales view
SET STATISTICS TIME ON;

-- Execute the query here

SET STATISTICS TIME OFF;
```

Comparing the execution times between these queries will help evaluate the performance impact of using the view versus direct joins and filters.

7. Simulate a situation where you need to store intermediate results during complex data manipulations. Use a temporary table 'TempResults' and demonstrate its application in a multi-step query process.

let's simulate a scenario where we perform a multi-step data manipulation process and store intermediate results in a temporary table named 'TempResults':

```
-- Create the TempResults temporary table
CREATE TABLE #TempResults (
    ID INT IDENTITY(1,1),
    ProductID INT,
    SaleAmount DECIMAL(10,2)
);

-- Step 1: Inserting intermediate results into TempResults
INSERT INTO #TempResults (ProductID, SaleAmount)
SELECT
    ProductID,
    SUM(Amount) AS TotalSales
FROM
    Sales
GROUP BY
    ProductID;
```

```sql
-- Step 2: Use the intermediate results in subsequent operations
SELECT
    t.ID,
    t.ProductID,
    t.SaleAmount,
    p.ProductName
FROM
    #TempResults t
INNER JOIN
    Products p ON t.ProductID = p.ProductID
WHERE
    t.SaleAmount > 1000;

-- Drop the temporary table when no longer needed
DROP TABLE #TempResults;
```

In this scenario:
1. We create a temporary table '#TempResults' with columns to hold intermediate results.
2. Step 1 involves calculating the total sale amounts per product from the 'Sales' table and inserting them into the temporary table.
3. Step 2 utilizes the stored intermediate results by joining with the 'Products' table to fetch additional details for products with sale amounts exceeding $1000.

Temporary tables like '#TempResults' are particularly useful for storing interim data during complex multi-step processes, enabling easier analysis and manipulation without affecting the original data. Once their use is complete, they can be dropped to free up space.

Experiment 9: Stored Procedures

Creating and Managing Stored Procedures:
1. Create a stored procedure that takes employee name as input and retrieves their department details.
2. Develop a stored procedure that calculates the total sales for a specific date range.
3. Alter an existing stored procedure to include error handling for cases where a record doesn't exist.

Solutions:
Here are the SQL examples for the requested stored procedures:

```
CREATE PROCEDURE GetEmployeeDepartmentDetails
    @EmployeeName NVARCHAR(50)
AS
BEGIN
    SELECT EmployeeName, Department
    FROM Employees
    WHERE EmployeeName = @EmployeeName;
END;
```

Stored Procedure to Calculate Total Sales for a Date Range:
This procedure calculates the total sales within a specific date range.

```
CREATE PROCEDURE CalculateTotalSalesForDateRange
    @StartDate DATE,
    @EndDate DATE
AS
BEGIN
    SELECT SUM(Amount) AS TotalSales
    FROM Sales
    WHERE SaleDate BETWEEN @StartDate AND @EndDate;
END;
```

Altering an Existing Stored Procedure for Error Handling:
Let's assume there's an existing procedure **InsertRecord** to insert data into a table, and we want to include error handling if the record doesn't exist.

```sql
-- Existing Procedure
CREATE PROCEDURE InsertRecord
    @ID INT,
    @Name NVARCHAR(50)
AS
BEGIN
    BEGIN TRY
        INSERT INTO YourTable (ID, Name) VALUES (@ID, @Name);
    END TRY
    BEGIN CATCH
        -- Add custom error handling/logic here
        PRINT 'Error: Record does not exist or other error occurred.';
    END CATCH
END;
```

These SQL examples showcase the creation of a procedure to retrieve employee details, calculate total sales, and the alteration of an existing procedure to include error handling for non-existent records. Adjust table and column names as per your database schema.

Practice Questions:

1. Create a stored procedure that fetches all employees' details from the 'Employee' table.

Here's an example of a basic stored procedure in SQL Server that retrieves all employee details from the 'Employee' table:

```sql
CREATE PROCEDURE GetAllEmployees
AS
BEGIN
    SET NOCOUNT ON; -- Suppress the message showing the number of rows affected

    SELECT * FROM Employee; -- Fetch all records from the Employee table
END;
```

This stored procedure named **GetAllEmployees** doesn't accept any parameters and simply retrieves all columns and rows from the 'Employee' table. When executed, it will return the entire set of employee details available in the table.

2. Develop a stored procedure that retrieves orders placed by a specific customer based on their ID.

Here's an example of a stored procedure that fetches orders by a specific customer ID:

```
CREATE PROCEDURE GetOrdersByCustomerID
    @CustomerID int
AS
BEGIN
    SET NOCOUNT ON;

    SELECT OrderID, OrderDate, TotalAmount
    FROM Orders
    WHERE CustomerID = @CustomerID;
END
```

This stored procedure **GetOrdersByCustomerID** takes a parameter **@CustomerID** and retrieves orders placed by that specific customer from the **Orders** table. Adjust the table and column names as per your database schema.

3. Write a procedure that updates the salary of employees based on their department, increasing it by a certain percentage.

Here's an example of a stored procedure that updates the salary of employees based on their department by increasing it by a certain percentage:

```
CREATE PROCEDURE UpdateSalaryByDepartment
    @DepartmentName NVARCHAR(50),
    @PercentageIncrease DECIMAL(5, 2)
AS
BEGIN
    SET NOCOUNT ON;

    UPDATE Employees
    SET Salary = Salary * (1 + @PercentageIncrease / 100)
    WHERE Department = @DepartmentName;
END
```

This stored procedure **UpdateSalaryByDepartment** takes two parameters: **@DepartmentName** to specify the department and **@PercentageIncrease** to define the percentage increase. Adjust the table and column names as per your database schema.

4. Create a procedure that retrieves orders along with customer details from related tables using joins.

Here's an example of a stored procedure that retrieves orders along with customer details from related tables using joins:

```
CREATE PROCEDURE GetOrdersWithCustomers
AS
BEGIN
    SET NOCOUNT ON;

    SELECT O.OrderID, O.OrderDate, C.CustomerName, C.Email
    FROM Orders O
    INNER JOIN Customers C ON O.CustomerID = C.CustomerID;
END
```

This stored procedure **GetOrdersWithCustomers** performs an **INNER JOIN** between the **Orders** and **Customers** tables on the **CustomerID** column to fetch order details alongside customer information. Adjust the table and column names based on your database schema.

5. Write a basic procedure to list countries in Asia, then make small changes to it

Create a stored procedure called **uspCountriesAsia** to list out all the countries with **ContinentId** equal to 1, in alphabetical order:

CountryName
China
India
Indonesia
Iran

As a reminder, the syntax of a basic stored procedure is:

```
CREATE PROC NameOfProcedure
  AS
-- now do something
SELECT ...
```

If you've got this working, modify the text of your query to create a different procedure called **uspCountriesEurope** which lists all the countries in continent id number 3, and check that this works.
Close down all your SQL Server Management Studio windows. Find the procedure called **uspCountriesAsia** in **Object Explorer**, and choose to modify it. Change the procedure so that it lists out the **CountryId** too:

CountryId	CountryName
19	China
24	India
9	Indonesia
37	Iran

Optionally save your query as **Basic procedures.sql**, then close it down.

6. Filter the select statement, only show events occuring in August.

The aim of this exercise is to create a stored procedure called **uspAugustEvents** which will show all events that occurred in the month of August:

EventID	EventName	EventDetails	EventDate
8	Hiroshima	United States	1995-08-06
20	Premier	First Season	1992-08-15
22	Attempt	1991 Soviet	1991-08-19
83	Slavery	Disgrace of slavery	1834-08-01
98	Economist	Bible of Absolute	1843-08-05

First write the SQL script which will retrieve event information for the month of August.

Now add the following code at the top of your query:

```
CREATE PROC NameOfProcedure
  AS
```

Replace the name of the procedure with **uspAugustEvents**, and then run the code to create it. Check that your procedure has been created:

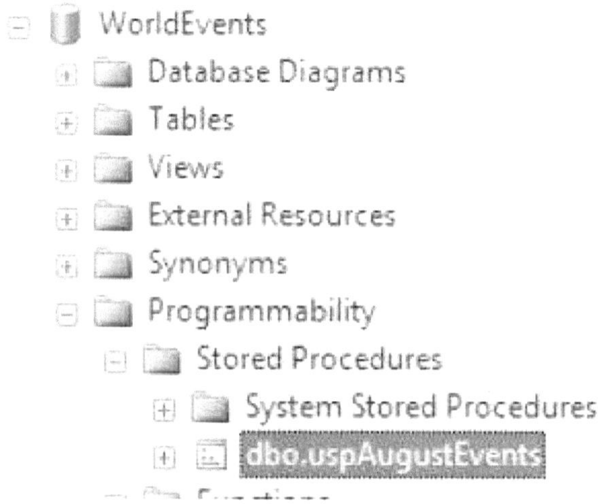

Optionally, save your SQL as **Nothing ever happens in August.sql,** then close it down.

7. Develop a procedure that inserts a new employee into the 'Employee' table with necessary validations.
Here's an example of a stored procedure that inserts a new employee into the 'Employee' table with necessary validations:

```sql
CREATE PROCEDURE InsertEmployee
    @EmpID INT,
    @EmpName VARCHAR(50),
    @DeptID INT,
    @Salary DECIMAL(10, 2)
AS
BEGIN
    SET NOCOUNT ON;

    IF EXISTS (SELECT 1 FROM Employee WHERE EmpID = @EmpID)
    BEGIN
        RAISEERROR('Employee ID already exists', 16, 1);
        RETURN;
    END

    IF @Salary < 0
    BEGIN
        RAISEERROR('Salary cannot be negative', 16, 1);
        RETURN;
    END

    INSERT INTO Employee (EmpID, EmpName, DeptID, Salary)
    VALUES (@EmpID, @EmpName, @DeptID, @Salary);

    SELECT 'Employee inserted successfully' AS Result;
END
```

This procedure **InsertEmployee** takes parameters for Employee ID (**@EmpID**), Employee Name (**@EmpName**), Department ID (**@DeptID**), and Salary (**@Salary**). It validates if the Employee ID already exists in the table and if the Salary is non-negative before inserting the new employee record into the 'Employee' table. Adjust the data types and validations as per your database schema requirements.

8. Write a procedure that deletes an order from the 'Order' table based on order ID.

Here's an example of a stored procedure that deletes an order from the 'Order' table based on the Order ID:

```sql
CREATE PROCEDURE DeleteOrder
    @OrderID INT
AS
BEGIN
    SET NOCOUNT ON;

    IF EXISTS (SELECT 1 FROM Orders WHERE OrderID = @OrderID)
    BEGIN
        DELETE FROM Orders WHERE OrderID = @OrderID;
        SELECT 'Order deleted successfully' AS Result;
    END
    ELSE
    BEGIN
        RAISEERROR('Order does not exist', 16, 1);
        RETURN;
    END
END
```

This procedure **DeleteOrder** takes a parameter for Order ID (**@OrderID**). It first checks if the order exists in the 'Orders' table based on the provided Order ID. If the order exists, it performs a deletion operation. Otherwise, it raises an error indicating that the order doesn't exist. Adjust the table and column names to match your database schema.

9. Create a procedure that updates the stock quantity of a product in the 'Inventory' table.

Here's an example of a stored procedure that updates the stock quantity of a product in the 'Inventory' table:

```sql
CREATE PROCEDURE UpdateStockQuantity
    @ProductID INT,
    @NewQuantity INT
AS
BEGIN
    SET NOCOUNT ON;

    IF EXISTS (SELECT 1 FROM Inventory WHERE ProductID = @ProductID)
    BEGIN
        UPDATE Inventory
        SET Quantity = @NewQuantity
        WHERE ProductID = @ProductID;

        SELECT 'Stock quantity updated successfully' AS Result;
    END
    ELSE
    BEGIN
        RAISEERROR('Product does not exist in inventory', 16, 1);
        RETURN;
    END
END
```

Sure, here's an example of a stored procedure in SQL Server that inserts a new employee into the 'Employee' table with necessary validations:

```
CREATE PROCEDURE InsertEmployee
    @EmployeeID INT,
    @EmployeeName NVARCHAR(50),
    @Department NVARCHAR(50),
    @Salary DECIMAL(10,2)
AS
BEGIN
    SET NOCOUNT ON;

    -- Check if the EmployeeID already exists
    IF EXISTS (SELECT 1 FROM Employee WHERE EmployeeID = @EmployeeID)
    BEGIN
        PRINT 'EmployeeID already exists. Choose a different EmployeeID.';
        RETURN;
    END

    -- Insert new employee if EmployeeID doesn't exist
    INSERT INTO Employee (EmployeeID, EmployeeName, Department, Salary)
    VALUES (@EmployeeID, @EmployeeName, @Department, @Salary);

    PRINT 'Employee inserted successfully';
END
```

This stored procedure, named **InsertEmployee**, takes parameters for EmployeeID, EmployeeName, Department, and Salary. It first checks if the provided EmployeeID already exists in the 'Employee' table. If the EmployeeID exists, it prints a message indicating the need for a different ID. Otherwise, it inserts the new employee details into the table and prints a success message. Adjust the data types and table/column names as per your schema.

10. Develop a procedure that transfers funds between two accounts, ensuring that it's an atomic transaction.

Here's an example of a stored procedure in SQL Server that transfers funds between two accounts while ensuring an atomic transaction:

```sql
CREATE PROCEDURE TransferFunds
    @FromAccount INT,
    @ToAccount INT,
    @Amount DECIMAL(10, 2)
AS
BEGIN
    SET NOCOUNT ON;
    BEGIN TRY
        BEGIN TRANSACTION; -- Start a transaction

        DECLARE @FromAccountBalance DECIMAL(10, 2);
        DECLARE @ToAccountBalance DECIMAL(10, 2);

        -- Fetch current balances of both accounts
        SELECT @FromAccountBalance = Balance FROM Accounts WHERE AccountID = @FromAccount;
        SELECT @ToAccountBalance = Balance FROM Accounts WHERE AccountID = @ToAccount;

        IF (@FromAccountBalance >= @Amount)
        BEGIN
            -- Deduct the amount from the sender's account
            UPDATE Accounts SET Balance = @FromAccountBalance - @Amount WHERE AccountID = @FromAccount;

            -- Add the amount to the recipient's account
            UPDATE Accounts SET Balance = @ToAccountBalance + @Amount WHERE AccountID = @ToAccount;

            COMMIT TRANSACTION; -- Commit the transaction
            PRINT 'Funds transferred successfully';
        END
        ELSE
        BEGIN
            ROLLBACK TRANSACTION; -- Rollback the transaction
            PRINT 'Insufficient balance in the sender''s account';
        END
    END TRY
    BEGIN CATCH
        IF @@TRANCOUNT > 0
            ROLLBACK TRANSACTION; -- Rollback the transaction in case of an error
        PRINT 'An error occurred. Transaction rolled back';
    END CATCH
END
```

This procedure **TransferFunds** takes three parameters: **@FromAccount** (sender's account), **@ToAccount** (recipient's account), and **@Amount** (amount to transfer). It first fetches the balances of both accounts and performs the transfer only if the sender's account has sufficient funds. The operation is wrapped in a transaction using **BEGIN TRANSACTION** and **COMMIT TRANSACTION**, ensuring that either both updates (deducting from sender and adding to the recipient) occur or none occur (using **ROLLBACK TRANSACTION** in case of insufficient balance or errors), thereby maintaining data integrity. Adjust the table/column names as per your schema.

11. Write a procedure that handles exceptions during data insertion and logs errors to an 'ErrorLog' table.

Below is an example of a stored procedure in SQL Server that inserts data into a table and logs any errors encountered during the process into an 'ErrorLog' table:

```sql
CREATE PROCEDURE InsertDataWithLogging
    @Param1 INT,
    @Param2 VARCHAR(50),
    @Param3 DECIMAL(18, 2)
AS
BEGIN
    SET NOCOUNT ON;

    BEGIN TRY
        INSERT INTO YourTable (Column1, Column2, Column3)
        VALUES (@Param1, @Param2, @Param3);

        PRINT 'Data inserted successfully';
    END TRY
    BEGIN CATCH
        DECLARE @ErrorMessage NVARCHAR(MAX) = ERROR_MESSAGE();
        DECLARE @ErrorSeverity INT = ERROR_SEVERITY();
        DECLARE @ErrorState INT = ERROR_STATE();

        INSERT INTO ErrorLog (ErrorMessage, ErrorSeverity, ErrorState)
        VALUES (@ErrorMessage, @ErrorSeverity, @ErrorState);

        PRINT 'An error occurred. Check ErrorLog for details';
    END CATCH
END
```

Replace **YourTable** with the actual table name where you want to insert the data. This stored procedure **InsertDataWithLogging** takes parameters **@Param1**, **@Param2**, and **@Param3** representing the data to be inserted. Inside the **TRY** block, it attempts to insert the data into the table. If an error occurs during the insertion process, the **CATCH** block captures the error message, severity, and state using **ERROR_MESSAGE()**, **ERROR_SEVERITY()**, and **ERROR_STATE()** respectively. It then inserts this error information into the 'ErrorLog' table. Adjust the column names and datatypes based on your requirements.

12. Create a procedure that calculates the total sales amount for a specific period and returns the total.

Below is an example of a stored procedure in SQL Server that calculates the total sales amount within a specific period:

```sql
CREATE PROCEDURE CalculateTotalSales
    @StartDate DATE,
    @EndDate DATE,
    @TotalSales DECIMAL(18, 2) OUTPUT
AS
BEGIN
    SET NOCOUNT ON;

    SELECT @TotalSales = SUM(Amount)
    FROM Sales
    WHERE SaleDate >= @StartDate AND SaleDate <= @EndDate;
END
```

This stored procedure **CalculateTotalSales** takes **@StartDate** and **@EndDate** parameters to specify the period and an **OUTPUT** parameter **@TotalSales** to return the calculated total sales amount. Adjust the table name, column names, and datatypes based on your database schema. To execute this procedure and retrieve the total sales amount:

```sql
DECLARE @Total DECIMAL(18, 2);
EXEC CalculateTotalSales '2023-01-01', '2023-12-31', @Total OUTPUT;
SELECT @Total AS TotalSales;
```

Replace **'2023-01-01'** and **'2023-12-31'** with the desired start and end dates of the period for which you want to calculate the total sales amount. Adjust the date format according to your date columns in the 'Sales' table.

13. Develop a procedure that calculates the average salary for employees within a particular department.

Here's an example of a stored procedure in SQL Server that calculates the average salary for employees within a specific department:

```sql
CREATE PROCEDURE CalculateAverageSalary
    @DepartmentID INT,
    @AverageSalary DECIMAL(18, 2) OUTPUT
AS
BEGIN
    SET NOCOUNT ON;

    SELECT @AverageSalary = AVG(Salary)
    FROM Employees
    WHERE DepartmentID = @DepartmentID;
END
```

This stored procedure **CalculateAverageSalary** takes **@DepartmentID** as a parameter to specify the department for which the average salary needs to be calculated. It uses an **OUTPUT** parameter **@AverageSalary** to return the calculated average salary. Modify the table name, column names, and datatypes as per your database schema.
To execute this procedure and retrieve the average salary:

```
DECLARE @AvgSalary DECIMAL(18, 2);
EXEC CalculateAverageSalary 123, @AvgSalary OUTPUT;
SELECT @AvgSalary AS AverageSalary;
```

Replace **123** with the department ID for which you want to calculate the average salary. Adjust the column names and conditions according to your 'Employees' table structure.

14. Write a procedure that uses a recursive CTE to fetch hierarchical data from an 'Organization' table.

Here's an example of a stored procedure using a recursive Common Table Expression (CTE) to fetch hierarchical data from an 'Organization' table:

```
CREATE PROCEDURE GetOrganizationHierarchy
AS
BEGIN
    SET NOCOUNT ON;

    WITH RecursiveCTE AS (
        SELECT OrganizationID, ParentID, OrgName, 0 AS Level
        FROM Organization
        WHERE ParentID IS NULL  -- Assuming NULL represents the top-level/root node

        UNION ALL

        SELECT o.OrganizationID, o.ParentID, o.OrgName, rc.Level + 1
        FROM Organization o
        INNER JOIN RecursiveCTE rc ON o.ParentID = rc.OrganizationID
    )
    SELECT OrganizationID, ParentID, OrgName, Level
    FROM RecursiveCTE
    ORDER BY Level, OrganizationID; -- Optional: Order by level and ID
END
```

This stored procedure **GetOrganizationHierarchy** uses a CTE to recursively fetch hierarchical data from the 'Organization' table. Adjust the table name, column names, and conditions according to your database schema. The CTE starts from the root node (where **ParentID** is **NULL**) and recursively retrieves child nodes.
To execute this procedure:

```
EXEC GetOrganizationHierarchy;
```

This will retrieve the hierarchical data from the 'Organization' table. Adjust the **ORDER BY** clause as needed to sort the results by the level and/or other columns.

15. Create a procedure that constructs dynamic SQL to fetch data from different tables based on user input

Here's an example of a stored procedure that constructs dynamic SQL to fetch data from different tables based on user input:

```
CREATE PROCEDURE FetchDataBasedOnInput
    @TableName NVARCHAR(100)
AS
BEGIN
    SET NOCOUNT ON;

    DECLARE @SQLQuery NVARCHAR(MAX);

    SET @SQLQuery = N'SELECT * FROM ' + QUOTENAME(@TableName);

    EXEC sp_executesql @SQLQuery;
END
```

This stored procedure **FetchDataBasedOnInput** takes a parameter **@TableName** that specifies the table name from which the data needs to be fetched. It constructs a dynamic SQL query using the input parameter and executes it using **sp_executesql**.
To execute this procedure:

```
EXEC FetchDataBasedOnInput @TableName = 'YourTableName';
```

Replace **'YourTableName'** with the actual table name from which you want to fetch the data. This procedure allows users to specify a table name dynamically, but ensure to handle user input properly to prevent SQL injection vulnerabilities.

16. Develop a procedure that uses temporary tables to store intermediate results during complex calculations.

Here's an example of a stored procedure that uses temporary tables to store intermediate results during complex calculations:

```sql
CREATE PROCEDURE ComplexCalculation
AS
BEGIN
    SET NOCOUNT ON;

    -- Create a temporary table to store intermediate results
    CREATE TABLE #TempResults (
        ID INT,
        Result DECIMAL(18, 2)
    );

    -- Perform some complex calculations and store results in the temporary table
    INSERT INTO #TempResults (ID, Result)
    SELECT ID, SomeComplexCalculationFunction(Column1, Column2)
    FROM YourTable;

    -- Fetch and work with the intermediate results
    SELECT *
    FROM #TempResults;

    -- Clean up the temporary table
    DROP TABLE #TempResults;
END
```

In this example, the **ComplexCalculation** stored procedure creates a temporary table **#TempResults** to store intermediate results. It performs complex calculations (represented by **SomeComplexCalculationFunction**) and inserts the results into the temporary table. It then retrieves and utilizes the stored intermediate results before dropping the temporary table.

Ensure to adapt **SomeComplexCalculationFunction** and **YourTable** to match your actual data and calculation requirements. Temporary tables are useful for handling interim data within complex procedures and can assist in breaking down complex operations into manageable steps.

17. Write a procedure that takes database backup and restores it to a specific point in time.

Performing database backup and point-in-time restoration involves SQL Server's built-in capabilities and requires administrative privileges. Here's an outline for a stored procedure that handles this process:

```
CREATE PROCEDURE BackupAndRestoreDatabase
    @BackupPath NVARCHAR(500),
    @DatabaseName NVARCHAR(100),
    @RestoreDateTime DATETIME
AS
BEGIN
    SET NOCOUNT ON;

    -- Step 1: Perform Database Backup
    DECLARE @BackupFileName NVARCHAR(500);
    SET @BackupFileName = @BackupPath + @DatabaseName + '_' +
    REPLACE(CONVERT(NVARCHAR(30), GETDATE(), 120), ':', '') + '.bak';

    BACKUP DATABASE @DatabaseName TO DISK = @BackupFileName;

    -- Step 2: Perform Point-in-Time Restoration
    DECLARE @RestoreSQL NVARCHAR(MAX);
    SET @RestoreSQL =
        'USE master; ' +
        'ALTER DATABASE [' + @DatabaseName + '] SET SINGLE_USER WITH ROLLBACK IMMEDIATE; ' +
        'RESTORE DATABASE [' + @DatabaseName + '] FROM DISK = ''' + @BackupFileName +
        ''' WITH FILE = 1, ' + 'RECOVERY, STOPAT = ''' + CONVERT(NVARCHAR(30), @RestoreDateTime, 121) +
        '''; ' + 'ALTER DATABASE [' + @DatabaseName + '] SET MULTI_USER;';

    EXEC(@RestoreSQL);
END
```

This stored procedure, **BackupAndRestoreDatabase**, accepts parameters for **@BackupPath** (where to save the backup), **@DatabaseName** (name of the database), and **@RestoreDateTime** (specific point in time for restoration). Please exercise caution when using this in a production environment, as database backups and restorations can affect critical data. Testing in a controlled environment is recommended before applying it in a live setting. Adjust the paths, permissions, and additional settings as required by your specific setup and security considerations.

Experiment 10: Triggers

Scenario:
You are working for a fictional company called "ABC Retailers." ABC Retailers manages an online store that sells various products. They have a database system to store their product information, customer details, and orders. To ensure data consistency and maintain specific business rules, triggers are employed in the database.

Database Schema:

1. Products Table:

Columns: ProductID (Primary Key), ProductName, QuantityAvailable, UnitPrice

2. Customers Table:

Columns: CustomerID (Primary Key), CustomerName, Email, MembershipTier

3. Orders Table:

Columns: OrderID (Primary Key), CustomerID (Foreign Key referencing Customers), ProductID (Foreign Key referencing Products), QuantityOrdered, TotalPrice, OrderDate

Tasks:

1. Trigger for Order Placement:
   Create a trigger named **UpdateProductQuantity** that automatically updates the **QuantityAvailable** in the **Products** table when a new order is placed. The trigger should reduce the **QuantityAvailable** by the **QuantityOrdered** for the specific product that has been ordered.
2. Trigger for Customer Tier Upgrade:
   Implement a trigger called **UpdateCustomerTier** that automatically upgrades a customer's membership tier based on their total purchase amount. If a customer's cumulative purchase amount exceeds $5000, upgrade their **MembershipTier** to 'Gold.' If it exceeds $3000, upgrade to 'Silver.' Otherwise, maintain 'Bronze.'
3. Trigger for Price Change:
   Create a trigger named **UpdateTotalPrice** that recalculates the **TotalPrice** in the **Orders** table when a product's **UnitPrice** is updated in the **Products** table. Ensure that the **TotalPrice** reflects the new **UnitPrice** for existing orders of that product.
4. Trigger for Order Validation:
   Implement a trigger named **ValidateOrder** that prevents the insertion of an order if the ordered quantity exceeds the available quantity in the **Products** table. If the order quantity is more than the available quantity, display an error message stating, "Insufficient quantity available for the order."
5. Trigger for Order Deletion:
   Create a trigger named **UpdateProductOnOrderDelete** that updates the **QuantityAvailable** in the **Products** table if an order is deleted. The trigger should increment the **QuantityAvailable** based on the quantity that was previously ordered and now deleted.
6. Trigger for Order Date Check:
   Implement a trigger named **CheckOrderDate** that ensures the **OrderDate** in the **Orders** table is not more than 30 days from the current date. If an order is placed with a future **OrderDate** beyond 30 days, display a warning message stating, "Order date cannot be more than 30 days in the future."

Solution:

SQL script to create the tables for the given scenario and insert some sample data:

```sql
-- Create Products Table
CREATE TABLE Products (
    ProductID INT PRIMARY KEY,
    ProductName VARCHAR(50),
    QuantityAvailable INT,
    UnitPrice DECIMAL(10, 2)
);

-- Insert sample data into Products Table
INSERT INTO Products (ProductID, ProductName, QuantityAvailable, UnitPrice)
VALUES
    (1, 'Product A', 100, 25.00),
    (2, 'Product B', 75, 35.50),
    (3, 'Product C', 50, 45.20),
    (4, 'Product D', 120, 20.75);

-- Create Customers Table
CREATE TABLE Customers (
    CustomerID INT PRIMARY KEY,
    CustomerName VARCHAR(50),
    Email VARCHAR(100),
    MembershipTier VARCHAR(20)
);
```

```sql
-- Insert sample data into Customers Table
INSERT INTO Customers (CustomerID, CustomerName, Email, MembershipTier)
VALUES
    (1, 'John Doe', 'john@example.com', 'Silver'),
    (2, 'Jane Smith', 'jane@example.com', 'Bronze'),
    (3, 'Michael Johnson', 'michael@example.com', 'Gold'),
    (4, 'Emily Davis', 'emily@example.com', 'Bronze');

-- Create Orders Table
CREATE TABLE Orders (
    OrderID INT PRIMARY KEY,
    CustomerID INT,
    ProductID INT,
    QuantityOrdered INT,
    TotalPrice DECIMAL(10, 2),
    OrderDate DATE,
    FOREIGN KEY (CustomerID) REFERENCES Customers(CustomerID),
    FOREIGN KEY (ProductID) REFERENCES Products(ProductID)
);

-- Insert sample data into Orders Table
INSERT INTO Orders (OrderID, CustomerID, ProductID, QuantityOrdered, TotalPrice, OrderDate)
VALUES
    (1, 1, 2, 5, 177.50, '2023-12-10'),
    (2, 3, 4, 8, 166.00, '2023-12-11'),
    (3, 2, 1, 3, 75.00, '2023-12-12'),
    (4, 4, 3, 2, 90.40, '2023-12-13');
```

This script will create the required tables (Products, Customers, Orders) and populate them with sample data reflecting the scenario of an online retail store. Adjust the data and schema as needed for specific requirements.

Trigger for Order Placement:

creating a trigger named **UpdateProductQuantity** in SQL Server that automatically updates the **QuantityAvailable** in the **Products** table when a new order is placed in the **Orders** table. The trigger will reduce the **QuantityAvailable** by the **QuantityOrdered** for the specific product that has been ordered:

```
-- Create the trigger
CREATE TRIGGER UpdateProductQuantity
ON Orders
AFTER INSERT
AS
BEGIN
    -- Update QuantityAvailable in Products table
    UPDATE Products
    SET QuantityAvailable = QuantityAvailable -
   (SELECT QuantityOrdered FROM inserted WHERE Products.ProductID = inserted.ProductID)
    FROM Products
    INNER JOIN inserted ON Products.ProductID = inserted.ProductID;
END;
```

This trigger will be activated after an **INSERT** operation on the **Orders** table. It calculates the new **QuantityAvailable** by subtracting the **QuantityOrdered** for the corresponding product in the **Products** table.

Trigger for Customer Tier Upgrade:

here's an example of how you can create a trigger to automatically update the membership tier of customers based on their total purchase amount:

```sql
-- Create the UpdateCustomerTier trigger
CREATE OR ALTER TRIGGER UpdateCustomerTier
ON Orders
AFTER INSERT
AS
BEGIN
    DECLARE @CustomerID INT;
    DECLARE @TotalPurchaseAmount DECIMAL(10, 2);

    SELECT @CustomerID = i.CustomerID
    FROM inserted i;

    SELECT @TotalPurchaseAmount = SUM(o.TotalPrice)
    FROM Orders o
    WHERE o.CustomerID = @CustomerID;

    IF (@TotalPurchaseAmount > 5000)
    BEGIN
        UPDATE Customers
        SET MembershipTier = 'Gold'
        WHERE CustomerID = @CustomerID;
    END
    ELSE IF (@TotalPurchaseAmount > 3000)
    BEGIN
        UPDATE Customers
        SET MembershipTier = 'Silver'
        WHERE CustomerID = @CustomerID;
    END
    ELSE
    BEGIN
        UPDATE Customers
        SET MembershipTier = 'Bronze'
        WHERE CustomerID = @CustomerID;
    END
END;
```

This trigger will activate after an insertion into the Orders table. It calculates the total purchase amount for the customer associated with the inserted order. Depending on the total purchase amount, it updates the membership tier of the customer in the Customers table accordingly.

Please test and adapt this code to fit your database schema and requirements accurately. Additionally, ensure to handle edge cases and exceptions as needed in a production environment.

Trigger for Price Change:

Here's an example of a trigger named **UpdateTotalPrice** that recalculates the **TotalPrice** in the **Orders** table when a product's **UnitPrice** is updated in the **Products** table:

```sql
-- Create Trigger for Price Change
CREATE TRIGGER UpdateTotalPrice ON Products
AFTER UPDATE OF UnitPrice
AS
BEGIN
    UPDATE Orders
    SET TotalPrice = (QuantityOrdered * i.UnitPrice)
    FROM Orders o
    JOIN inserted i ON o.ProductID = i.ProductID
    JOIN deleted d ON o.ProductID = d.ProductID
    WHERE d.UnitPrice <> i.UnitPrice;
END;
```

This trigger fires after an update on the **UnitPrice** column of the **Products** table (**AFTER UPDATE OF UnitPrice**). It performs an update on the **TotalPrice** in the **Orders** table where the **UnitPrice** of the affected products has changed. Please note that this is a basic example, and you might need to adjust the logic or enhance it based on your specific requirements and database structure.

Trigger for Order Validation:

Here's an example of how you can create a trigger named **ValidateOrder** in SQL Server to prevent the insertion of an order if the ordered quantity exceeds the available quantity in the Products table:

```sql
-- Create Trigger for Order Validation
CREATE TRIGGER ValidateOrder
ON Orders
AFTER INSERT
AS
BEGIN
    SET NOCOUNT ON;

    DECLARE @ProductID INT, @QuantityOrdered INT, @AvailableQuantity INT;

    -- Get the ProductID and QuantityOrdered from the inserted rows
    SELECT @ProductID = i.ProductID, @QuantityOrdered = i.QuantityOrdered
    FROM inserted i;

    -- Get the available quantity of the product
    SELECT @AvailableQuantity = QuantityAvailable
    FROM Products
    WHERE ProductID = @ProductID;

    -- Check if the ordered quantity exceeds the available quantity
    IF (@QuantityOrdered > @AvailableQuantity)
    BEGIN
        RAISEERROR('Insufficient quantity available for the order', 16, 1);
        ROLLBACK TRANSACTION; -- Rollback the transaction to prevent the insertion
    END
END;
```

Explanation:

1. This trigger is defined on the **Orders** table and fires after an **INSERT** operation.
2. It retrieves the **ProductID** and **QuantityOrdered** from the **inserted** pseudo table (representing the rows being inserted).
3. Then, it fetches the available quantity (**QuantityAvailable**) from the **Products** table based on the **ProductID**.
4. If the **QuantityOrdered** is greater than the **QuantityAvailable**, it raises an error message using **RAISEERROR** and rolls back the transaction, preventing the insertion.

Please note:
1. Ensure that the trigger is created in the appropriate database where the **Orders** and **Products** tables exist.
2. Adjust the column names and table references based on your actual schema if they differ from the provided scenario.

Trigger for Order Deletion:

Here's an example of a trigger in SQL Server that updates the **QuantityAvailable** in the **Products** table when an order is deleted:

```
CREATE TRIGGER UpdateProductOnOrderDelete
ON Orders
AFTER DELETE
AS
BEGIN
    DECLARE @DeletedOrderID INT;
    DECLARE @DeletedQuantity INT;
    DECLARE @DeletedProductID INT;

    SELECT @DeletedOrderID = deleted.OrderID,
           @DeletedQuantity = deleted.QuantityOrdered,
           @DeletedProductID = deleted.ProductID
    FROM deleted;

    IF (@DeletedOrderID IS NOT NULL)
    BEGIN
        UPDATE Products
        SET QuantityAvailable = QuantityAvailable + @DeletedQuantity
        WHERE ProductID = @DeletedProductID;
    END
END;
```

This trigger is set to execute after a row is deleted from the **Orders** table. It retrieves the **OrderID**, **QuantityOrdered**, and **ProductID** of the deleted order. Then, it updates the **QuantityAvailable** in the **Products** table by adding the quantity previously ordered and now deleted back to the available stock.
Please note that triggers can have significant impacts on database performance, especially when dealing with large datasets. Ensure thorough testing and consider potential side effects before implementing triggers in a production environment.

Trigger for Order Date Check:

Here's an example of a trigger implementation named **CheckOrderDate** for the scenario described:

```
-- Create the trigger
CREATE OR REPLACE TRIGGER CheckOrderDate
BEFORE INSERT ON Orders
FOR EACH ROW
DECLARE
    FutureDate DATE;
BEGIN
    FutureDate := SYSDATE + 30; -- Calculate future date

    IF :NEW.OrderDate > FutureDate THEN
        RAISE_APPLICATION_ERROR(-20001, 'Order date cannot be more than 30 days in the future');
    END IF;
END;
```

This trigger is set to execute before an insertion operation on the **Orders** table. It checks if the **OrderDate** provided in the **INSERT** statement is within the allowed 30-day window from the current date (**SYSDATE**). If the **OrderDate** is beyond 30 days in the future, it raises an application error with the specified message.

Please note that the exact implementation might vary based on the database system used (the syntax provided is for Oracle PL/SQL). Adjustments might be necessary for different database systems such as SQL Server or MySQL.

Experiment 11: Transaction

Scenario: Suppose you are responsible for managing a financial database for a banking institution. The database stores information about customer transactions. Due to the critical nature of financial data, it's essential to maintain data integrity and handle potential errors.

Tasks:

1. Error Handling: Create a stored procedure named **InsertTransaction** that inserts transaction details into a **Transactions** table. Implement error handling mechanisms to ensure data consistency and log errors to an **ErrorLog** table.

2. Transactions: Develop a stored procedure named **TransferFunds** that facilitates transferring funds between accounts. Ensure the transfer is atomic, and if any part of the transaction fails, roll back the entire operation.

3. Questions:

4. Demonstrate the process of handling errors during the insertion of a transaction record using the **InsertTransaction** procedure. Show how the error is logged in the **ErrorLog** table.

5. Simulate a fund transfer between two accounts using the **TransferFunds** procedure. Execute the transfer within a transaction block and demonstrate the rollback mechanism if an error occurs during the transfer.

Solution:

You're tasked with managing a financial database for a banking institution that stores information about customer transactions. Ensuring data integrity and handling errors are crucial aspects of managing this financial data.

Task:

1. Error Handling in InsertTransaction Procedure: Create a stored procedure named **InsertTransaction** that inserts transaction details into a **Transactions** table. Implement error handling mechanisms within this procedure to ensure data consistency and log errors to an **ErrorLog** table.

The **InsertTransaction** procedure should perform the following:

1. Insert transaction details (e.g., TransactionID, CustomerID, TransactionAmount, TransactionDate) into the **Transactions** table.
2. Implement error handling using TRY...CATCH blocks to capture exceptions that might occur during the insertion process.
3. In case of an error (e.g., constraint violations, data truncation), log details about the error, including error message, timestamp, and the attempted transaction details, into an **ErrorLog** table.
4. Ensure that the error log includes relevant information to identify the source of the error and the transaction that caused it.

Here's an example of how you might implement the **InsertTransaction** stored procedure in SQL Server with error handling using **TRY...CATCH** blocks:

```sql
-- Create ErrorLog table if not exists
IF NOT EXISTS (SELECT * FROM sys.objects WHERE object_id = OBJECT_ID(N'ErrorLog') AND type in (N'U'))
BEGIN
    CREATE TABLE ErrorLog (
        ErrorLogID INT PRIMARY KEY IDENTITY(1,1),
        ErrorMessage NVARCHAR(MAX),
        ErrorTimestamp DATETIME,
        TransactionID INT,
        CustomerID INT,
        TransactionAmount DECIMAL(18,2),
        TransactionDate DATE
    );
END
GO

-- Create InsertTransaction procedure
CREATE PROCEDURE InsertTransaction
    @TransactionID INT,
    @CustomerID INT,
    @TransactionAmount DECIMAL(18,2),
    @TransactionDate DATE
```

```sql
AS
BEGIN
    BEGIN TRY
        -- Attempt to insert transaction details
        INSERT INTO Transactions (TransactionID, CustomerID, TransactionAmount, TransactionDate)
        VALUES (@TransactionID, @CustomerID, @TransactionAmount, @TransactionDate);
    END TRY
    BEGIN CATCH
        -- Log error details to ErrorLog table
        INSERT INTO ErrorLog (ErrorMessage, ErrorTimestamp, TransactionID, CustomerID, TransactionAmount, TransactionDate)
        VALUES (ERROR_MESSAGE(), GETDATE(), @TransactionID, @CustomerID, @TransactionAmount, @TransactionDate);

        -- Throw the error (optional: you can handle the error further here)
        THROW;
    END CATCH
END
GO
```

This script creates an **ErrorLog** table to store error details and a **InsertTransaction** stored procedure that attempts to insert transaction details into a **Transactions** table. If an error occurs during the insertion process, it catches the error, logs the details into the **ErrorLog** table, and rethrows the error to be handled further up the chain.
Remember to adjust the data types and constraints according to your specific database schema. Also, ensure proper permissions are set for executing the stored procedure and writing to the tables.

1. TransferFunds Procedure: Develop a stored procedure named **TransferFunds** that allows transferring funds between accounts within the banking database.
The **TransferFunds** procedure should perform the following steps within a transaction:
1. Accept parameters like SourceAccountID, DestinationAccountID, and TransferAmount.
2. Begin a transaction to ensure the operation is atomic and consistent.
3. Deduct **TransferAmount** from the balance of the **SourceAccountID**.
4. Add TransferAmount to the balance of the DestinationAccountID.
5. Commit the transaction if both debit and credit operations are successful.

6. If any part of the transaction encounters an error (e.g., insufficient funds, invalid accounts), rollback the entire operation to maintain data consistency.
Ensure that the procedure handles exceptions and errors gracefully, rolling back the transaction if necessary, and maintaining data integrity within the financial database.

Creating a robust **TransferFunds** procedure in SQL Server involves handling transactional operations and ensuring data integrity. Here's an example of how you might implement it:

```
-- Create TransferFunds procedure
CREATE PROCEDURE TransferFunds
    @SourceAccountID INT,
    @DestinationAccountID INT,
    @TransferAmount DECIMAL(18,2)
AS
BEGIN
    BEGIN TRY
        BEGIN TRANSACTION; -- Begin the transaction

        -- Check if SourceAccountID has enough balance
        DECLARE @SourceBalance DECIMAL(18,2);
        SELECT @SourceBalance = Balance FROM Accounts WHERE AccountID = @SourceAccountID;

        IF @SourceBalance < @TransferAmount
        BEGIN
            -- If insufficient funds, raise an error and rollback the transaction
            RAISEERROR('Insufficient funds in the source account.', 16, 1);
        END

        -- Deduct TransferAmount from the source account
        UPDATE Accounts
        SET Balance = Balance - @TransferAmount
        WHERE AccountID = @SourceAccountID;
```

```
        -- Add TransferAmount to the destination account
        UPDATE Accounts
        SET Balance = Balance + @TransferAmount
        WHERE AccountID = @DestinationAccountID;

        COMMIT TRANSACTION; -- If everything is successful, commit the transaction
    END TRY
    BEGIN CATCH
        -- If any error occurs, rollback the transaction
        IF @@TRANCOUNT > 0
            ROLLBACK TRANSACTION;

        -- Log the error
        INSERT INTO ErrorLog (ErrorMessage, ErrorTimestamp, SourceAccountID, DestinationAccountID, TransferAmount)
        VALUES (ERROR_MESSAGE(), GETDATE(), @SourceAccountID, @DestinationAccountID, @TransferAmount);

        -- Throw the error (optional: you can handle the error further here)
        THROW;
    END CATCH
END
```

This procedure begins a transaction and then performs the necessary debit and credit operations within the **Accounts** table. It first checks if the source account has sufficient funds; if not, it raises an error and rolls back the transaction. If all operations succeed, it commits the transaction. However, if any part of the transaction encounters an error, it rolls back the entire transaction and logs the error details into the **ErrorLog** table.

1. Ensure to adapt the table names, column names, and constraints as per your database schema. Also, it's essential to grant appropriate permissions for executing the procedure and modifying the necessary tables.
2. Implement the InsertTransaction procedure:
3. Create the **InsertTransaction** procedure to insert transaction details into the **Transactions** table.
4. Implement error handling mechanisms using **TRY-CATCH** to catch and handle exceptions.
5. Log any errors encountered during the insertion process into the **ErrorLog** table.

Execution Scenario for Part A:

1. Simulate the execution of the **InsertTransaction** procedure with invalid data or a scenario where an error occurs during the insertion.
2. Verify that the error is caught, and the details are logged in the **ErrorLog** table.
3. Implement the TransferFunds procedure:
4. Develop the **TransferFunds** procedure to facilitate fund transfers between accounts within a transaction block.
5. Incorporate error handling and the **TRY-CATCH** block to manage exceptions.
6. Ensure that in case of an error during the fund transfer, the entire transaction is rolled back.

Execution Scenario for Part B:

1. Simulate a fund transfer between two accounts using the **TransferFunds** procedure.
2. Execute the transfer within a transaction and introduce a scenario where an error occurs during the transfer.
3. Verify that the entire transaction is rolled back, and no incomplete or erroneous changes are committed.

For Part a, let's start with implementing the **InsertTransaction** procedure that handles errors using **TRY...CATCH** blocks and logs any encountered errors into the **ErrorLog** table.

```sql
-- Create ErrorLog table if not exists
IF NOT EXISTS (SELECT * FROM sys.objects WHERE object_id = OBJECT_ID(N'ErrorLog') AND type in (N'U'))
BEGIN
    CREATE TABLE ErrorLog (
        ErrorLogID INT PRIMARY KEY IDENTITY(1,1),
        ErrorMessage NVARCHAR(MAX),
        ErrorTimestamp DATETIME,
        TransactionID INT,
        CustomerID INT,
        TransactionAmount DECIMAL(18,2),
        TransactionDate DATE
    );
END
GO

-- Create InsertTransaction procedure
CREATE PROCEDURE InsertTransaction
    @TransactionID INT,
    @CustomerID INT,
    @TransactionAmount DECIMAL(18,2),
    @TransactionDate DATE
AS
BEGIN
    BEGIN TRY
        -- Attempt to insert transaction details
        INSERT INTO Transactions (TransactionID, CustomerID, TransactionAmount, TransactionDate)
        VALUES (@TransactionID, @CustomerID, @TransactionAmount, @TransactionDate);
    END TRY
    BEGIN CATCH
        -- Log error details to ErrorLog table
        INSERT INTO ErrorLog (ErrorMessage, ErrorTimestamp, TransactionID, CustomerID, TransactionAmount, TransactionDate)
        VALUES (ERROR_MESSAGE(), GETDATE(), @TransactionID, @CustomerID, @TransactionAmount, @TransactionDate);

        -- Throw the error (optional: you can handle the error further here)
        THROW;
    END CATCH
END
GO
```

For Part b, let's implement the **TransferFunds** procedure which will handle fund transfers between accounts within a transaction block, ensuring rollback in case of errors:

```sql
-- Create TransferFunds procedure
CREATE PROCEDURE TransferFunds
    @SourceAccountID INT,
    @DestinationAccountID INT,
    @TransferAmount DECIMAL(18,2)
AS
BEGIN
    BEGIN TRY
        BEGIN TRANSACTION; -- Begin the transaction

        -- Check if SourceAccountID has enough balance
        DECLARE @SourceBalance DECIMAL(18,2);
        SELECT @SourceBalance = Balance FROM Accounts WHERE AccountID = @SourceAccountID;

        IF @SourceBalance < @TransferAmount
        BEGIN
            -- If insufficient funds, raise an error and rollback the transaction
            RAISEERROR('Insufficient funds in the source account.', 16, 1);
        END

        -- Deduct TransferAmount from the source account
        UPDATE Accounts
        SET Balance = Balance - @TransferAmount
        WHERE AccountID = @SourceAccountID;

        -- Add TransferAmount to the destination account
        UPDATE Accounts
        SET Balance = Balance + @TransferAmount
        WHERE AccountID = @DestinationAccountID;

        COMMIT TRANSACTION; -- If everything is successful, commit the transaction
    END TRY
    BEGIN CATCH
        -- If any error occurs, rollback the transaction
        IF @@TRANCOUNT > 0
            ROLLBACK TRANSACTION;

        -- Log the error
        INSERT INTO ErrorLog (ErrorMessage, ErrorTimestamp, SourceAccountID, DestinationAccountID, TransferAmount)
        VALUES (ERROR_MESSAGE(), GETDATE(), @SourceAccountID, @DestinationAccountID, @TransferAmount);

        -- Throw the error (optional: you can handle the error further here)
        THROW;
    END CATCH
END
GO
```

To simulate errors and ensure that error handling works as expected, you can execute these procedures with invalid data or scenarios that would trigger errors. For instance, attempting to insert a transaction with duplicate TransactionID or trying to transfer funds with an amount greater than the source account balance can trigger errors that will be caught by the **TRY...CATCH** blocks and logged into the **ErrorLog** table.

Practice Questions:

1. Develop a stored procedure that performs an INSERT operation into a table. Implement error handling to capture exceptions like constraint violations or data truncation.

Here's an example of a stored procedure that performs an INSERT operation into a table and handles errors using **TRY...CATCH** blocks to capture exceptions such as constraint violations or data truncation:

```
CREATE PROCEDURE InsertRecord
    @Param1 INT,
    @Param2 NVARCHAR(50),
    @Param3 DATE
AS
BEGIN
    BEGIN TRY
        INSERT INTO YourTableName (Column1, Column2, Column3)
        VALUES (@Param1, @Param2, @Param3);
    END TRY
    BEGIN CATCH
        -- Log the error or handle it as needed
        DECLARE @ErrorMessage NVARCHAR(MAX);
        DECLARE @ErrorSeverity INT;
        DECLARE @ErrorState INT;

        SELECT
            @ErrorMessage = ERROR_MESSAGE(),
            @ErrorSeverity = ERROR_SEVERITY(),
            @ErrorState = ERROR_STATE();

        -- Log the error details into an ErrorLog table or perform other actions
        INSERT INTO ErrorLog (ErrorMessage, ErrorSeverity, ErrorState, Parameter1, Parameter2, Parameter3)
        VALUES (@ErrorMessage, @ErrorSeverity, @ErrorState, @Param1, @Param2, @Param3);

        -- Optionally, re-throw the error or perform specific error handling
        THROW;
    END CATCH
END
```

Replace **YourTableName** with the actual name of your table and adjust the column names and data types accordingly. This procedure takes parameters **@Param1**, **@Param2**, and **@Param3** as inputs to perform the INSERT operation. Inside the **TRY** block, it attempts to execute the INSERT statement. If any error occurs during the execution, it goes to the **CATCH** block. Within the **CATCH** block, you can retrieve error details using the **ERROR_MESSAGE()**, **ERROR_SEVERITY()**, and **ERROR_STATE()** functions and log these details into an **ErrorLog** table or perform any specific error handling required for your scenario.
Remember to adjust the error logging mechanism or handling according to your specific needs, such as logging additional information or taking different actions based on the encountered errors.

2. Create a stored procedure to update multiple rows in a table within a transaction. If an update for any row fails, ensure a rollback for the entire operation.

Here's an example of a stored procedure that updates multiple rows in a table within a transaction and ensures a rollback if any update fails:

```sql
CREATE PROCEDURE UpdateMultipleRows
    @Param1 INT,
    @Param2 NVARCHAR(50)
AS
BEGIN
    BEGIN TRANSACTION;

    BEGIN TRY
        -- Update rows based on certain conditions
        UPDATE YourTableName
        SET ColumnToUpdate = @Param2
        WHERE SomeCondition = @Param1; -- Define your condition for updating rows

        -- Check if any rows were affected
        IF @@ROWCOUNT = 0
        BEGIN
            -- If no rows were updated, raise an error
            RAISEERROR('No rows were updated.', 16, 1);
        END

        -- If everything is successful, commit the transaction
        COMMIT TRANSACTION;
    END TRY

    BEGIN CATCH
        -- If any error occurs, rollback the transaction
        IF @@TRANCOUNT > 0
            ROLLBACK TRANSACTION;

        -- Log the error or perform specific error handling
        DECLARE @ErrorMessage NVARCHAR(MAX);
        DECLARE @ErrorSeverity INT;
        DECLARE @ErrorState INT;

        SELECT
            @ErrorMessage = ERROR_MESSAGE(),
            @ErrorSeverity = ERROR_SEVERITY(),
            @ErrorState = ERROR_STATE();

        -- Log the error details into an ErrorLog table or perform other actions
        INSERT INTO ErrorLog (ErrorMessage, ErrorSeverity, ErrorState, Parameter1, Parameter2)
        VALUES (@ErrorMessage, @ErrorSeverity, @ErrorState, @Param1, @Param2);

        -- Optionally, re-throw the error or perform specific error handling
        THROW;
    END CATCH
END
```

Replace **YourTableName** with the actual name of your table. This procedure takes parameters **@Param1** and **@Param2** as inputs to define conditions for updating rows.

Inside the **TRY** block, it attempts to update rows based on certain conditions. If the update affects zero rows, it raises an error using **RAISEERROR()**. In the **CATCH** block, it rolls back the transaction if any error occurs during the update process, logs the error details into an **ErrorLog** table, and throws the error.
You can modify the update conditions and error handling mechanism as per your specific use case. Adjust the columns and conditions in the **UPDATE** statement to suit your table's structure and the criteria for updating rows.

3. Simulate a deadlock scenario between two transactions accessing the same table. Write SQL statements that create a deadlock situation and demonstrate deadlock handling mechanisms.

To create a deadlock scenario, we'll simulate two transactions that try to update rows in a table, resulting in a deadlock situation. I'll use two SQL connections to simulate this scenario.

In SQL Connection 1:

```
-- Begin Transaction 1
BEGIN TRANSACTION;

-- Update statement in Transaction 1
UPDATE YourTableName
SET ColumnToUpdate = 'NewValue'
WHERE ID = 1;

-- Wait for some time (don't commit yet)
WAITFOR DELAY '00:00:05';

-- In another query window or SQL Connection 2,
--execute the following statements after Transaction 1 starts but before it's committed
-- Begin Transaction 2

BEGIN TRANSACTION;

-- Update statement in Transaction 2
UPDATE YourTableName
SET ColumnToUpdate = 'AnotherNewValue'
WHERE ID = 2;

-- Wait for some time (don't commit yet)
WAITFOR DELAY '00:00:05';

-- Now, in the first query window or SQL Connection 1,
--execute the following statements after Transaction 2 starts but before it's committed

-- Try to update the row affected by Transaction 2
UPDATE YourTableName
SET ColumnToUpdate = 'UpdatedByTransaction1'
WHERE ID = 2; -- Same row as Transaction 2 is trying to update

-- This should result in a deadlock scenario

-- Commit Transaction 1 (to allow Transaction 2 to proceed and encounter a deadlock)
COMMIT TRANSACTION;
```

In SQL Connection 2 (before Transaction 1 commits):

```sql
-- Begin Transaction 2
BEGIN TRANSACTION;

-- Update statement in Transaction 2
UPDATE YourTableName
SET ColumnToUpdate = 'AnotherNewValue'
WHERE ID = 2;

-- Wait for some time (don't commit yet)
WAITFOR DELAY '00:00:05';

-- Go back to the first query window or SQL Connection 1 to continue the process
```

This setup creates a scenario where Transaction 1 and Transaction 2 are both trying to update rows in the same table. When Transaction 1 tries to update a row that Transaction 2 has locked and Transaction 2 tries to update a row that Transaction 1 has locked, a deadlock occurs.
SQL Server's deadlock handling mechanism will automatically detect and resolve the deadlock by terminating one of the transactions involved in the deadlock, allowing the other transaction to continue.
You might notice that the code is intentionally causing a deadlock situation. Deadlocks are undesirable and should be avoided in production systems. Various strategies, such as proper indexing, minimizing transaction lengths, and optimizing queries, can help prevent or minimize deadlock occurrences.

4. Design a stored procedure that logs errors encountered during database operations into an ErrorLog table. Include details like error message, timestamp, and operation type.

Here's an example of a stored procedure that logs errors encountered during database operations into an **ErrorLog** table. It captures details such as error message, timestamp, and operation type:

```sql
CREATE PROCEDURE LogError
    @ErrorMessage NVARCHAR(MAX),
    @OperationType NVARCHAR(50)
AS
BEGIN
    DECLARE @ErrorTimestamp DATETIME = GETDATE();

    BEGIN TRY
        -- Begin a transaction to ensure atomicity of the logging process
        BEGIN TRANSACTION;

        -- Insert the error details into the ErrorLog table
        INSERT INTO ErrorLog (ErrorMessage, ErrorTimestamp, OperationType)
        VALUES (@ErrorMessage, @ErrorTimestamp, @OperationType);

        -- Commit the transaction if the insertion is successful
        COMMIT TRANSACTION;
    END TRY
    BEGIN CATCH
        -- If an error occurs during the logging process, rollback the transaction
        IF @@TRANCOUNT > 0
            ROLLBACK TRANSACTION;

        -- Log the error to SQL Server's error log or perform alternative error handling
        -- Use PRINT or other means to log the error message to SQL Server's error log

        -- Optionally, re-throw the error or perform specific error handling
        THROW;
    END CATCH
END
```

This procedure **LogError** takes **@ErrorMessage** (the error message encountered during the operation) and **@OperationType** (type of operation, such as 'INSERT', 'UPDATE', 'DELETE', etc.) as parameters.

Within a **TRY...CATCH** block, it attempts to insert the error details into the **ErrorLog** table. If the insertion succeeds, the transaction is committed. If any error occurs during the logging process, it rolls back the transaction and optionally logs the error to SQL Server's error log or handles the error in an alternative way.
Replace the **ErrorLog** table with your actual error log table name and adjust the columns and data types as needed to suit your requirements. Also, consider adding more columns or details to the error log table based on the information you want to capture.

5. Develop a script involving nested transactions. Execute a set of SQL statements within a parent transaction and a child transaction. Display the impact when rolling back each transaction.

Nested transactions can be demonstrated by executing a set of SQL statements within a parent transaction and a child transaction. Rolling back each transaction will show their individual impacts.

```
-- Create a table for demonstration purposes
CREATE TABLE DemoTable (
    ID INT PRIMARY KEY,
    Value NVARCHAR(50)
);

-- Begin the parent transaction
BEGIN TRANSACTION ParentTransaction;

-- Insert a record into the table within the parent transaction
INSERT INTO DemoTable (ID, Value)
VALUES (1, 'ParentTransaction');

-- Begin the child transaction
BEGIN TRANSACTION ChildTransaction;

-- Insert another record into the table within the child transaction
INSERT INTO DemoTable (ID, Value)
VALUES (2, 'ChildTransaction');

-- Rollback the child transaction
ROLLBACK TRANSACTION ChildTransaction;

-- Rollback the parent transaction
ROLLBACK TRANSACTION ParentTransaction;

-- Select records from the table to view the impact
SELECT * FROM DemoTable;
```

In this script:
1. A table **DemoTable** is created for demonstration purposes.
2. A parent transaction **ParentTransaction** is started.
3. Within the parent transaction, a record is inserted into **DemoTable**.
4. Then, a child transaction **ChildTransaction** is started within the parent transaction.

5. Within the child transaction, another record is inserted into **DemoTable**.
6. The child transaction is explicitly rolled back (**ROLLBACK TRANSACTION ChildTransaction**).
7. Finally, the parent transaction is rolled back (**ROLLBACK TRANSACTION ParentTransaction**).
After executing these statements, you'll see that both records inserted within the transactions will be rolled back. When you **SELECT * FROM DemoTable** after the script execution, you'll find that the table is empty as both transactions have been rolled back, and the changes were not committed.

6. Create a stored procedure that throws custom error messages based on specific business rules or conditions. Test the procedure with various scenarios to validate error messages.

Here's an example of a stored procedure in SQL Server that incorporates custom error messages based on specific business rules or conditions:

```
CREATE PROCEDURE ValidateTransaction
    @amount DECIMAL,
    @accountBalance DECIMAL
AS
BEGIN
    IF @amount <= 0
    BEGIN
        RAISERROR('Invalid transaction amount. Amount must be greater than zero.', 16, 1)
        RETURN
    END

    IF @amount > @accountBalance
    BEGIN
        RAISERROR('Insufficient funds. Transaction amount exceeds available balance.', 16, 2)
        RETURN
    END

    -- Additional business rules or conditions can be added here

    -- If all conditions pass, execute the transaction logic
    -- Your transaction logic goes here
    PRINT 'Transaction successful!'
END
```

This procedure **ValidateTransaction** takes in an **@amount** and **@accountBalance**. It checks two conditions: if the amount is less than or equal to zero and if the amount exceeds the account balance. In both cases, it raises custom error messages with different severity levels using **RAISERROR**.
To test this procedure, you can execute it with various scenarios:

```
-- Test scenarios
DECLARE @balance DECIMAL = 1000

EXEC ValidateTransaction @amount = 500, @accountBalance = @balance
-- Output: Transaction successful!

EXEC ValidateTransaction @amount = 0, @accountBalance = @balance
-- Output: Msg 50000, Level 16, State 1, Line 10
-- Invalid transaction amount. Amount must be greater than zero.

EXEC ValidateTransaction @amount = 1500, @accountBalance = @balance
-- Output: Msg 50001, Level 16, State 2, Line 14
-- Insufficient funds. Transaction amount exceeds available balance.
```

Adjust the scenarios by changing the **@amount** and **@accountBalance** values to validate the error messages and the success message based on different conditions and business rules.

7. Design a stored procedure that involves inserting data into tables linked with foreign key constraints. Implement error handling to address scenarios where foreign key constraints are violated.

Here's an example of a stored procedure that involves inserting data into tables linked with foreign key constraints and handles errors related to these constraints:
Let's say we have two tables: **Orders** and **OrderDetails** linked by a foreign key constraint.

```
CREATE TABLE Orders (
    OrderID INT PRIMARY KEY,
    OrderDate DATE
);

CREATE TABLE OrderDetails (
    DetailID INT PRIMARY KEY,
    OrderID INT FOREIGN KEY REFERENCES Orders(OrderID),
    ProductName NVARCHAR(50),
    Quantity INT
);
```

Now, let's create a stored procedure **InsertOrderDetails** that inserts data into the **OrderDetails** table while handling foreign key constraint violations:

```sql
CREATE PROCEDURE InsertOrderDetails
    @OrderID INT,
    @ProductName NVARCHAR(50),
    @Quantity INT
AS
BEGIN
    BEGIN TRY
        BEGIN TRANSACTION

        -- Check if the OrderID exists in the Orders table
        IF NOT EXISTS (SELECT 1 FROM Orders WHERE OrderID = @OrderID)
        BEGIN
            THROW 50001, 'Invalid OrderID. Order does not exist.', 1
        END

        -- Insert into OrderDetails if the OrderID exists
        INSERT INTO OrderDetails (DetailID, OrderID, ProductName, Quantity)
        VALUES ((SELECT ISNULL(MAX(DetailID), 0)
        + 1 FROM OrderDetails), @OrderID, @ProductName, @Quantity)

        COMMIT TRANSACTION
        PRINT 'Order details inserted successfully!'
    END TRY
    BEGIN CATCH
        IF @@TRANCOUNT > 0
            ROLLBACK TRANSACTION

        DECLARE @ErrorMessage NVARCHAR(500)
        DECLARE @ErrorSeverity INT
        DECLARE @ErrorState INT

        SELECT
            @ErrorMessage = ERROR_MESSAGE(),
            @ErrorSeverity = ERROR_SEVERITY(),
            @ErrorState = ERROR_STATE()

        RAISERROR(@ErrorMessage, @ErrorSeverity, @ErrorState)
    END CATCH
END
```

This stored procedure **InsertOrderDetails** checks if the provided **OrderID** exists in the **Orders** table before inserting into the **OrderDetails** table. If the **OrderID** doesn't exist, it throws a custom error message. If the **OrderID** exists, it proceeds with the insertion into **OrderDetails**.

Here's an example of how you might use this stored procedure:

```
-- Test scenarios
EXEC InsertOrderDetails @OrderID = 1001, @ProductName = 'Product A', @Quantity = 5
-- Output: Order details inserted successfully!

EXEC InsertOrderDetails @OrderID = 999, @ProductName = 'Product B', @Quantity = 3
-- Output: Msg 50001, Level 16, State 1
-- Invalid OrderID. Order does not exist.
```

Modify the parameters in the **EXEC** statements to test the procedure by inserting order details with both valid and invalid **OrderID** values, ensuring the error handling for foreign key constraint violations works as expected.

8. Explore different isolation levels like READ COMMITTED, READ UNCOMMITTED, REPEATABLE READ, and SERIALIZABLE. Write queries to illustrate the behavior of each isolation level.

Isolation levels control how transactions interact with each other regarding visibility and consistency of data. Let's explore different isolation levels in SQL Server using queries to demonstrate their behaviors.

READ COMMITTED

```
-- Session 1
BEGIN TRANSACTION
SELECT * FROM Orders -- Will not block

-- Session 2
BEGIN TRANSACTION
UPDATE Orders SET OrderDate = GETDATE() WHERE OrderID = 1
-- Will block until Session 1's transaction completes or releases the locks
COMMIT
```

In READ COMMITTED isolation level, a transaction sees only committed data. Concurrent transactions can read but not modify data locked by other transactions until the locking transaction is committed.

READ UNCOMMITTED

```
-- Session 1
SET TRANSACTION ISOLATION LEVEL READ UNCOMMITTED
BEGIN TRANSACTION
SELECT * FROM Orders
-- May read uncommitted changes made by other transactions
```

In READ UNCOMMITTED isolation level, a transaction can read uncommitted changes made by other transactions, risking seeing inconsistent or dirty data.

REPEATABLE READ

```sql
-- Session 1
SET TRANSACTION ISOLATION LEVEL REPEATABLE READ
BEGIN TRANSACTION
SELECT * FROM Orders WHERE OrderDate > '2023-01-01'
-- Will not see rows inserted after the transaction began

-- Session 2
BEGIN TRANSACTION
INSERT INTO Orders (OrderID, OrderDate) VALUES (1002, '2023-12-31')
-- Will be blocked until Session 1's transaction completes or releases locks
```

In REPEATABLE READ isolation level, a transaction sees a consistent snapshot of the database at the start of the transaction. It prevents other transactions from inserting new rows that match the query criteria until the current transaction is complete.

SERIALIZABLE

```sql
-- Session 1
SET TRANSACTION ISOLATION LEVEL SERIALIZABLE
BEGIN TRANSACTION
SELECT * FROM Orders WHERE OrderID = 1
-- Places a range lock on the row to prevent other
--transactions from inserting new rows that might
--satisfy the WHERE condition
```

In SERIALIZABLE isolation level, transactions acquire range locks, preventing other transactions from inserting new rows within the range of the query conditions until the current transaction is complete.
You can test and observe these isolation levels' behaviors by executing the provided queries in separate sessions or by altering the isolation levels and observing how they affect concurrent transactions and data visibility.

9. Implement a script that uses savepoints within a transaction. Show how savepoints can help in rolling back specific parts of a transaction instead of the entire transaction.

Savepoints allow you to mark specific points within a transaction, providing a way to roll back to a particular savepoint rather than the entire transaction. Let's create a script that demonstrates the use of savepoints in SQL Server:

```sql
-- Create sample tables
CREATE TABLE Employee (
    EmployeeID INT PRIMARY KEY,
    Name NVARCHAR(50),
    Salary DECIMAL(10, 2)
);

-- Insert sample data
INSERT INTO Employee (EmployeeID, Name, Salary)
VALUES (1, 'John Doe', 50000),
       (2, 'Jane Smith', 60000),
       (3, 'Alice Johnson', 70000);

-- Begin a transaction with savepoints
BEGIN TRANSACTION;

-- Insert a new employee
INSERT INTO Employee (EmployeeID, Name, Salary)
VALUES (4, 'Mark Anderson', 65000);

-- Savepoint 1: Mark the point after inserting the new employee
SAVE TRANSACTION Savepoint1;

-- Attempt to update salary for an employee that doesn't exist (Intentional error)
UPDATE Employee SET Salary = 75000 WHERE EmployeeID = 5;

-- Savepoint 2: Mark the point after the update attempt
SAVE TRANSACTION Savepoint2;

-- Insert another new employee
INSERT INTO Employee (EmployeeID, Name, Salary)
VALUES (5, 'Emily Brown', 55000);

-- Commit the transaction
COMMIT;
```

In this script, we begin a transaction and perform multiple actions. Savepoints are set at different stages within the transaction (**Savepoint1** and **Savepoint2**). If an error occurs, we can rollback to a specific savepoint to undo changes made after that point without rolling back the entire transaction.
Now, let's demonstrate rolling back to a savepoint:

```sql
-- Check the current state of the Employee table
SELECT * FROM Employee;
-- Output: Shows the records including John Doe, Jane Smith,
--Alice Johnson, Mark Anderson, and Emily Brown

-- Rollback to Savepoint2 to undo the update and insertion after Savepoint2
ROLLBACK TRANSACTION Savepoint2;

-- Check the Employee table after rolling back to Savepoint2
SELECT * FROM Employee;
-- Output: Shows the records including John Doe, Jane Smith, Alice Johnson, and Mark Anderson;
--Emily Brown's insertion after Savepoint2 is rolled back
```

The rollback to **Savepoint2** removes the changes made after **Savepoint2**, allowing you to selectively undo portions of the transaction while preserving changes made before that savepoint.

10. Develop a stored procedure containing DML operations within a TRY...CATCH block. Execute the procedure with invalid data to observe how errors are caught and handled.

Here's an example of a stored procedure that performs DML (Data Manipulation Language) operations within a TRY...CATCH block to handle errors gracefully:

```sql
CREATE PROCEDURE ProcessData
    @EmployeeID INT,
    @NewSalary DECIMAL(10, 2)
AS
BEGIN
    BEGIN TRY
        BEGIN TRANSACTION;

        -- Update the salary for the specified employee
        UPDATE Employee SET Salary = @NewSalary WHERE EmployeeID = @EmployeeID;

        -- Intentional error: Attempt to update a non-existing column (to simulate an error)
        UPDATE Employee SET NonExistingColumn = 0 WHERE EmployeeID = @EmployeeID;

        COMMIT TRANSACTION;
        PRINT 'Data processed successfully!';
    END TRY
    BEGIN CATCH
        IF @@TRANCOUNT > 0
            ROLLBACK TRANSACTION;

        DECLARE @ErrorMessage NVARCHAR(4000) = ERROR_MESSAGE();
        DECLARE @ErrorSeverity INT = ERROR_SEVERITY();
        DECLARE @ErrorState INT = ERROR_STATE();

        RAISERROR(@ErrorMessage, @ErrorSeverity, @ErrorState);
    END CATCH
END
```

This stored procedure **ProcessData** takes an **EmployeeID** and a **NewSalary** as parameters and attempts to update the salary of the specified employee. However, intentionally, it also attempts to update a non-existing column to trigger an error within the TRY block.

Now, let's execute the procedure with invalid data to observe how errors are caught and handled:

```
EXEC ProcessData @EmployeeID = 5, @NewSalary = 75000;
-- Output:
-- Msg 207, Level 16, State 1
-- Invalid column name 'NonExistingColumn'.
```

Executing this will result in an error being caught by the CATCH block due to the attempt to update a non-existing column. The procedure catches the error, rolls back the transaction, and raises the caught error message.

Feel free to adjust the **EmployeeID** or provide different invalid data to observe how the TRY...CATCH block handles various errors encountered during the execution of the stored procedure.

Experiment 12: Viva Questions and Answers

1. **What is a primary key?**
   Answer: A primary key is a column or set of columns that uniquely identifies each row in a table. It enforces uniqueness and ensures that no two rows can have the same values in the primary key column(s).
2. **Differentiate between CHAR and VARCHAR data types in SQL Server.**
   Answer: CHAR is a fixed-length string data type, while VARCHAR is a variable-length string data type. CHAR columns require padding with spaces to reach the defined length, whereas VARCHAR columns store only the actual data length.
3. **Explain the purpose of the WHERE clause in SQL.**
   Answer: The WHERE clause is used to filter rows based on specified conditions in SQL queries. It allows you to retrieve only the rows that meet the specified criteria.
4. **What is the difference between DELETE and TRUNCATE commands?**
   Answer: DELETE is a DML (Data Manipulation Language) command used to remove specific rows from a table based on conditions, allowing the use of a WHERE clause. TRUNCATE is a DDL (Data Definition Language) command that removes all rows from a table without using conditions and reset's identity columns.
5. **Explain the purpose of the GROUP BY clause.**
   Answer: The GROUP BY clause is used with aggregate functions (such as SUM, COUNT, AVG) to group rows that share the same values in specified columns. It helps in performing aggregate operations on these grouped rows.
6. **What is a foreign key?**
   Answer: A foreign key is a column or set of columns that establishes a relationship between two tables. It refers to the primary key in another table, enforcing referential integrity between related tables.
7. **Differentiate between INNER JOIN and LEFT JOIN.**
   Answer: INNER JOIN returns only the rows that have matching values in both tables based on the specified condition. LEFT JOIN retrieves all rows from the left table and the matched rows from the right table. If there is no match, NULL values are returned for the right table's columns.
8. **What is the purpose of the HAVING clause?**
   Answer: The HAVING clause is used in conjunction with the GROUP BY clause to filter rows based on aggregate conditions. It applies conditions to grouped rows after the GROUP BY operation.
9. **Explain the purpose of an index in a database.**
   Answer: An index is a database object that improves the speed of data retrieval operations on a table. It allows for faster data access by creating an ordered structure based on specified columns, reducing the time required to search for and retrieve data.
10. **What are stored procedures?**
    Answer: Stored procedures are precompiled SQL statements stored in the database that can be executed with a single command. They are reusable, enhance security, and improve performance by reducing network traffic.
11. **How does the ACID property ensure data integrity in database transactions?**
    Answer: ACID (Atomicity, Consistency, Isolation, Durability) ensures data integrity in transactions. Atomicity ensures that transactions are all-or-nothing, Consistency maintains data integrity, Isolation ensures transactions are independent, and Durability guarantees that committed transactions persist even in the event of system failures.
12. **Explain the difference between a clustered index and a non-clustered index.**
    Answer: A clustered index determines the physical order of data rows in a table based on the indexed column(s). In contrast, a non-clustered index creates a separate structure that points to the physical locations of data rows, leaving the table's data order unchanged.
13. **What is normalization in database design?**
    Answer: Normalization is the process of organizing data in a database to reduce redundancy and dependency. It involves breaking down large tables into smaller ones and establishing relationships to ensure data integrity.
14. **Explain the purpose of the SQL CASE statement.**
    Answer: The CASE statement in SQL is used to perform conditional logic within queries. It evaluates conditions and returns a value based on the first condition that is true, similar to an IF-THEN-ELSE statement.
15. **What is the difference between UNION and UNION ALL?**

Answer: UNION merges the results of two or more SELECT queries and removes duplicate rows, while UNION ALL also merges the results but retains all rows, including duplicates.

16. **How do you handle NULL values in SQL queries?**
    Answer: NULL values can be handled using functions like IS NULL, IS NOT NULL to check for NULL values, COALESCE to replace NULL values with another value, or using the IFNULL function (in some SQL implementations).
17. **Explain the purpose of the TOP clause in SQL Server.**
    Answer: The TOP clause is used to limit the number of rows returned by a query. It specifies the maximum number of rows to be returned from the query result set.
18. **What is a view in SQL Server?**
    Answer: A view is a virtual table based on the result set of a SELECT query. It doesn't store data itself but presents data from one or more tables as if it were a table.
19. **Explain the purpose of the ROLLUP and CUBE operators in SQL Server.**
    Answer: ROLLUP and CUBE are operators used in conjunction with GROUP BY to generate subtotals and grand totals in query result sets. ROLLUP produces subtotals along specified columns, while CUBE generates subtotals for all combinations of columns.
20. **How can you improve SQL query performance?**
    Answer: Query performance can be improved by creating indexes, optimizing SQL queries, minimizing the use of SELECT *, avoiding unnecessary JOINs, and using appropriate data types and normalization techniques. Additionally, optimizing database design and using stored procedures can enhance performance.
21. **Explain the purpose of a transaction in SQL Server.**
    Answer: A transaction in SQL Server represents a sequence of one or more SQL operations treated as a single logical unit. It ensures the atomicity, consistency, isolation, and durability (ACID properties) of database operations.
22. **Differentiate between a view and a table in SQL Server.**
    Answer: A table is a physical structure that stores data, while a view is a virtual table generated from the result of a SELECT query and doesn't store data directly. Views are based on one or more tables and provide a customized presentation of data.
23. **Explain the purpose of the EXISTS operator in SQL Server.**
    Answer: The EXISTS operator is used in SQL queries to check the existence of rows returned by a subquery. It returns true if the subquery returns at least one row; otherwise, it returns false.
24. **What is the purpose of the ROW_NUMBER() function in SQL Server?**
    Answer: The ROW_NUMBER() function assigns a unique sequential integer to each row returned by a query based on specified ordering criteria. It's often used to generate row numbers for result sets.
25. **Explain the difference between the UNION and UNION ALL operators.**
    Answer: UNION merges the results of two or more SELECT queries, removing duplicate rows, while UNION ALL merges results but retains all rows, including duplicates.
26. **What is a trigger in SQL Server?**
    Answer: A trigger in SQL Server is a database object that automatically executes in response to specific events (e.g., INSERT, UPDATE, DELETE) occurring on a table. It is used to enforce business rules, maintain data integrity, or automate actions based on data changes.
27. **How do you add a new column to an existing table in SQL Server?**
    Answer: You can add a new column to an existing table using the ALTER TABLE statement:
    ```
    ALTER TABLE TableName
    ADD NewColumnName DataType;
    ```
28. **Explain the purpose of the MAX() and MIN() aggregate functions in SQL Server.**
    Answer: MAX() returns the maximum value from a column, while MIN() returns the minimum value. They are used with GROUP BY or independently to find the maximum or minimum value in a dataset.
29. **What is the purpose of the SET NOCOUNT ON statement in SQL Server stored procedures?**
    Answer: SET NOCOUNT ON suppresses the message indicating the number of rows affected by a SQL statement. It improves performance by reducing network traffic.
30. **Explain the difference between a clustered and non-clustered index.**
    Answer: A clustered index determines the physical order of rows in a table based on the indexed column(s), while a non-clustered index creates a separate structure that points to the physical locations of data rows.
31. **What is the purpose of the TOP clause in SQL Server?**

Answer: The TOP clause is used to limit the number of rows returned by a query. It specifies the maximum number of rows to be returned from the query result set.

32. **Explain the purpose of the SQL Server function DATEDIFF().**
    Answer: DATEDIFF() calculates the difference between two dates in terms of a specified date part (e.g., days, months, years). It returns an integer representing the difference.
33. **How can you optimize SQL queries for better performance?**
    Answer: Query optimization can be achieved by using appropriate indexes, avoiding unnecessary JOINs, optimizing WHERE clauses, limiting the use of SELECT *, and ensuring efficient data types usage.
34. **What is a deadlock in SQL Server?**
    Answer: A deadlock occurs when two or more transactions are waiting indefinitely for resources held by each other, preventing progress. SQL Server automatically resolves deadlocks by rolling back one of the transactions to allow others to proceed.
35. **Explain the purpose of the COALESCE() function in SQL Server.**
    Answer: COALESCE() returns the first non-null value from a list of expressions. It's used to handle NULL values by substituting them with alternative non-null values.
36. **What is the purpose of the UNIQUE constraint in SQL Server?**
    Answer: The UNIQUE constraint ensures that all values in a column or a combination of columns are unique, allowing no duplicate values within the specified scope.
37. **Explain the purpose of the SQL Server function CONVERT().**
    Answer: CONVERT() is used to convert data from one data type to another. It's often used to format dates, numbers, and strings into different representations.
38. **What is the purpose of the ROLLBACK statement in SQL Server transactions?**
    Answer: ROLLBACK is used to undo changes made within a transaction and restores the database to its state before the transaction began.
39. **Explain the purpose of the LIKE operator in SQL Server.**
    Answer: The LIKE operator is used in a WHERE clause to search for a specified pattern within a column. It allows the use of wildcard characters (% and _) to match patterns.
40. **What is the purpose of the UNIQUEIDENTIFIER data type in SQL Server?**
    Answer: UNIQUEIDENTIFIER is a data type used to store a globally unique identifier (GUID) value in SQL Server. It generates unique identifiers that are globally unique across databases and tables.
41. **Explain the purpose of the ROW_NUMBER() function in SQL Server.**
    Answer: The ROW_NUMBER() function assigns a unique sequential integer to each row returned by a query based on specified ordering criteria. It's often used for pagination or ranking purposes.
42. **Differentiate between a stored procedure and a user-defined function (UDF) in SQL Server.**
    Answer: A stored procedure is a set of SQL statements that perform a specific task or operation. It can contain DML and DDL statements. A UDF is a reusable function that returns a value and cannot contain DML statements but can be used within queries.
43. **Explain the purpose of the TRIGGER_NESTLEVEL() function in SQL Server triggers.**
    Answer: TRIGGER_NESTLEVEL() returns the nesting level of the current trigger execution. It's used to determine the level of nesting when triggers are called recursively.
44. **What is the purpose of the COALESCE() function in SQL Server?**
    Answer: COALESCE() returns the first non-null value from a list of expressions. It's used to handle NULL values by substituting them with alternative non-null values.
45. **Differentiate between the CHARINDEX() and PATINDEX() functions in SQL Server.**
    Answer: CHARINDEX() returns the starting position of a substring within a string, while PATINDEX() returns the starting position of a pattern within a string using wildcard characters.
46. **Explain the purpose of the SQL Server function FORMAT().**
    Answer: FORMAT() is used to format the value of an expression into a specific format, such as date, time, currency, or numeric formats, based on a format pattern.
47. **What is the purpose of the @@IDENTITY system function in SQL Server?**
    Answer: @@IDENTITY returns the last identity value generated in the current session within the current scope. It's often used to retrieve the last inserted identity value into a table with an identity column.
48. **Differentiate between a clustered and non-clustered index in SQL Server.**
    Answer: A clustered index determines the physical order of rows in a table based on the indexed column(s). In contrast, a non-clustered index creates a separate structure that points to the physical locations of data rows.
49. **Explain the purpose of the SQL Server function IIF().**

Answer: IIF() is a shorthand function used to perform a conditional operation in SQL Server. It evaluates a specified condition and returns one of two specified values based on the evaluation.

50. **What is the purpose of the CHECK constraint in SQL Server?**
    Answer: The CHECK constraint enforces the validity of data entered into a column by defining a condition that each row must satisfy. It restricts the values that can be inserted or updated based on the specified condition.
51. **Explain the difference between UNION and UNION ALL operators in SQL Server.**
    Answer: UNION merges the results of two or more SELECT queries and removes duplicate rows, while UNION ALL merges results but retains all rows, including duplicates.
52. **What is the purpose of the XML data type in SQL Server?**
    Answer: The XML data type in SQL Server allows storing and manipulating XML data within a column. It enables XML-based operations, such as querying and modifying XML data.
53. **Explain the purpose of the TRY_CONVERT() function in SQL Server.**
    Answer: TRY_CONVERT() attempts to convert a value to a specified data type. If the conversion fails, it returns NULL instead of throwing an error, allowing handling of conversion issues.
54. **Differentiate between DELETE and TRUNCATE commands in SQL Server.**
    Answer: DELETE is a DML (Data Manipulation Language) command used to remove specific rows from a table based on conditions, allowing the use of a WHERE clause. TRUNCATE is a DDL (Data Definition Language) command that removes all rows from a table without conditions and resets identity columns.
55. **What is the purpose of the SQL Server function STUFF()?**
    Answer: STUFF() is used to replace a specified sequence of characters in a string with another set of characters. It's commonly used to update or manipulate string values.
56. **Explain the purpose of the SQL Server function DATEADD().**
    Answer: DATEADD() is used to add or subtract a specified time interval (such as days, months, years) to a date or time value, returning a new date or time.
57. **What is the purpose of the ROWLOCK hint in SQL Server?**
    Answer: ROWLOCK hint instructs SQL Server to acquire row-level locks instead of page-level or table-level locks. It helps in minimizing the lock contention and resource utilization.
58. **Explain the purpose of the CROSS APPLY operator in SQL Server.**
    Answer: CROSS APPLY is used to invoke a table-valued function for each row returned by a query and join the results of the function with the outer query.
59. **What is the purpose of the SQL Server function DATEPART()?**
    Answer: DATEPART() extracts a specific part (such as year, month, day) from a date or time value and returns the extracted part as an integer.
60. **Explain the difference between CHAR and VARCHAR data types in SQL Server.**
    Answer: CHAR is a fixed-length string data type, while VARCHAR is a variable-length string data type. CHAR columns require padding with spaces to reach the defined length, whereas VARCHAR columns store only the actual data length.
61. **What is the purpose of the SQL Server function RANK()?**
    Answer: RANK() is a window function used to assign a rank to each row in a result set based on a specified ordering. It can handle ties and assigns the same rank to identical values.
62. **Differentiate between the INNER JOIN and OUTER JOIN in SQL Server.**
    Answer: INNER JOIN retrieves rows when there is a match in both tables based on the specified join condition. OUTER JOIN retrieves rows from both tables, and if there's no match, it includes NULL values for columns from the table without a match.
63. **Explain the purpose of the SQL Server function ISNULL().**
    Answer: ISNULL() replaces NULL values with a specified replacement value. It's used to handle NULL values in expressions or columns.
64. **What is the purpose of the SET NOCOUNT ON statement in SQL Server stored procedures?**
    Answer: SET NOCOUNT ON suppresses the message indicating the number of rows affected by a SQL statement. It improves performance by reducing network traffic.
65. **Explain the purpose of the SQL Server function DATEPART().**
    Answer: DATEPART() extracts a specific part (such as year, month, day) from a date or time value and returns the extracted part as an integer.
66. **What is the purpose of the SQL Server function LEN()?**
    Answer: LEN() returns the number of characters in a string or the number of bytes required to store a variable. It's used to determine the length of a string value.

67. **Explain the difference between the GROUP BY and PARTITION BY clauses in SQL Server.**
    Answer: GROUP BY is used to group rows that share the same values in specified columns and perform aggregate functions on these groups. PARTITION BY is used with window functions to partition the result set into subsets based on specified criteria.
68. **What is the purpose of the SQL Server function LTRIM()?**
    Answer: LTRIM() removes leading spaces from a string value. It's used to eliminate leading spaces in character values.
69. **Explain the purpose of the SQL Server function CAST().**
    Answer: CAST() is used to convert a value from one data type to another by specifying the target data type. It allows data type conversions between compatible types.
70. **What is the purpose of the SQL Server function REPLACE()?**
    Answer: REPLACE() is used to replace occurrences of a specified substring within a string with another substring. It's commonly used to perform string replacements.
71. **Explain the purpose of the SQL Server function AVG().**
    Answer: AVG() calculates the average value of a set of numeric values within a specified column. It's used to determine the average of numerical data.
72. **What is the purpose of the SQL Server function UPPER()?**
    Answer: UPPER() converts all characters in a string to uppercase. It's used to ensure consistency in case-sensitive comparisons.
73. **Explain the difference between the EXISTS and IN operators in SQL Server.**
    Answer: EXISTS is used to check for the existence of rows returned by a subquery, while IN is used to check if a value matches any value in a list of values.
74. **What is the purpose of the SQL Server function STUFF()?**
    Answer: STUFF() is used to replace a specified sequence of characters in a string with another set of characters. It's commonly used to update or manipulate string values.
75. **Explain the purpose of the SQL Server function LOWER().**
    Answer: LOWER() converts all characters in a string to lowercase. It's used to ensure consistency in case-sensitive comparisons.

ONLINE RESOURCES

Mock Viva voce video

Link https://youtu.be/K2jYIlIwwNM?si=NiM5TC8FzE9dJEvN

QR Code

ADDITIONAL RESOURCE

YouTube Video Links –

Introduction of My SQL -https://youtu.be/-7NOhrJoDko
Introduction To Microsoft SQL Server- https://youtu.be/ea8J7PsfaEc
DBMS Introduction- https://youtu.be/SwB6RTAQ-o0
Microsoft Access – Quick Introduction: https://youtu.be/oilEviyIOpo